HOW CPA FIRMS WORK: THE BUSINESS OF PUBLIC ACCOUNTING

Marc Rosenberg, CPA

MONOGRAPHS BY MARC ROSENBERG

CPA Firm Management & Governance

CPA Firm Succession Planning: A Perfect Storm

How to Bring In New Partners

How to Negotiate a CPA Firm Merger

Strategic Planning & Goal Setting for Results

How to Operate a Compensation Committee

What Really *Makes CPA Firms Profitable?*

Guide to Planning the Firm Retreat

Effective Partner Relations and Communications

For more information or to purchase additional titles visit:
www.rosenbergassoc.com + click on
"Monographs by Marc Rosenberg"

Connect with Marc:
marc@rosenbergassoc.com
blog.rosenbergassoc.com

HOW CPA FIRMS WORK: THE BUSINESS OF PUBLIC ACCOUNTING

Marc Rosenberg, CPA

Copyright ©2013
The Rosenberg Associates Ltd.
1000 Skokie Boulevard, Suite 555
Wilmette, IL 60091

TABLE OF CONTENTS

TABLE OF CONTENTS

1

Introduction

"Engaging your employees -- involving them in the business -- can drive revenue growth. An educated workforce can also make better decisions, work more efficiently, and seize opportunities faster. Teaching your employees to be smart businesspeople can be a big investment, but it's one that can have a significant return."

Keith Lamb, Inc. Magazine

Personnel in <u>any</u> organization, from widget manufacturers to hospitals to baseball teams to charities, work with more enthusiasm and commitment when they genuinely feel part of the organization. When people understand how they fit in the overall scheme and grasp the essentials of how the organization operates, they produce higher quality work and are more energized. CPA firms are no exception.

Throughout over 20 years of consulting to CPA firms, I have observed hundreds of CPA firm training programs and new employee orientations. But there is one major subject that is consistently missing: staff training in the *business* of running a CPA firm.

<u>Who will benefit from reading this monograph?</u>

Primary group: New staff joining your firm. The <u>primary</u> use of this monograph is to teach staff, especially those going through the firm's new employee orientation process, about the business of public accounting.

Interns. The curriculum at university accounting programs focuses 99% on technical accounting and tax subjects. Students learn virtually nothing about how CPA firms work, how to advance their careers and what makes firms successful. Since internships are now the number one method used by firms to recruit college graduates, this monograph is a great opportunity to expose your future employees, relatively early in their accounting careers, to the CPA firm industry.

Experienced staff. Making sure that your *existing* staff understands the basics of the CPA industry and the firm itself will help reinforce what they have been exposed to throughout their tenure with the firm.

Partners. We are quite sure that partners – yes, partners - who read this monograph will learn a lot about the CPA industry and even about their own firm that they didn't know.

Administrative staff. Countless surveys and interviews of administrative staff have revealed that their biggest gripe is being made to feel like "second-class citizens." This usually isn't intentional. It's just that CPA firms are very busy places and are very client-centric. As a result, client service personnel often don't take the time to explain to admin staff why their work is so important and how it fits in to the overall scheme of things. Their occasional rudeness to admin staff may further the problem.

This monograph will provide your admin team with a new perspective on the business of CPA firms - i.e., how their functions contribute to the firm's success and profitability.

What you will learn from reading this monograph

1. Current trends in the CPA profession.
2. Demographics of the industry.
3. What CPA firms do.
4. How CPA firms measure their performance.
5. How CPA firms are managed and organized.
6. How CPA firms get clients and keep them.
7. The tremendously impressive list of innovations that have taken place in CPA firms over the past 20 years.
8. What attracts staff to firms and what it takes to retain them.
9. What it takes to be a successful staff person at a CPA firm.
10. How staff advance at a CPA firm.
11. Reputation of CPAs compared to other professions.
12. CPA firm economics: what makes firms profitable...and what holds back the bottom line.
13. The 25 Best Practices of well-managed firms.
14. Computer software commonly used by CPA firms.

2

Pop Quiz

It would be interesting to hear how people would answer a number of very basic questions about the CPA firm industry <u>before</u> they read the rest of this monograph.

If, for the fun of it, you give this quiz to a group of personnel, I strongly suggest that you do it in this manner:

Give each person 6 blank pieces of paper. Ask everyone to write the answers to each of the questions below on one of the sheets. Then, go over each question and ask people to hold their answers, just like on a television quiz show. The session leader should take a few moments to write down the responses given by the various people.

Another alternative is to have people complete this quiz and turn them in to be graded.

Either approach avoids simply reading off the questions and asking for a show of hands. This causes people to respond to peer pressure and makes it impossible to get an honest polling.

The following quizzes address basic, fundamental information. It's very valuable to gauge the group's knowledge or perception of these issues before a new employee orientation program begins.

Two Pop Quizzes follow:
- For staff.
- For partners.

See the Appendix for the correct answers.

5

POP QUIZ FOR <u>STAFF</u>
CPA INDUSTRY ISSUES

1. For over 30 years, the Gallup organization has conducted periodic polls of the public's perception of the honesty & ethics of various professions. How do accountants compare to other professions?

	Public's Perception of Accountants vs. Other Professio		
	Accountants Are Higher	Accountants About the Same	Accountar Are Lowe
Bankers			
Journalists			
Lawyers			
Stock brokers			

2. What is the hottest management issue in the CPA profession today?

3. How many total work hours (includes overtime, non-billable time, sick, vacation and holiday time) does the average <u>staff</u> person at a CPA firm work?

4. How many total work hours (includes overtime, non-billable time, sick, vacation and holiday time) does the average <u>partner</u> at a CPA firm work?

5. What is the average annual income of a typical equity partner at a <u>local</u> CPA firm?

6. What is the single most important skill, talent or attribute that it takes to become a partner at a CPA firm?

6

POP QUIZ FOR <u>PARTNERS</u>
CPA INDUSTRY ISSUES

1. The Gallup organization periodically polls the public's perception of the honesty and ethics of various professions. How do you think accountants compare to other professions?

	Public's Perception of Accountants vs. Other Professions		
	Accountants Are Higher	Accountants About the Same	Accountants Are Lower
Bankers			
Journalists			
Lawyers			
Stock brokers			

2. Name 3 "game-changing" innovations in the CPA firm industry during the past 20 years <u>besides</u> technology:

   _____

   _____

   _____

3. Name 3 critical trends in the CPA firm industry today. Only list management issues, not technical accounting and tax issues.

   _____

   _____

   _____

4. The <u>best and easiest</u> opportunity to increase revenues for most local multi-partner firms is (check only one):
   [ ] Referral sources
   [ ] Advertising, PR and branding
   [ ] Existing clients

5. The strongest correlation with firm profitability is (check only one):
   [ ] Overhead spending   [ ] Partner charge hours
   [ ] Staff charge hours   [ ] Fees per partner

6. Which of the following are among the <u>most important</u> factors in <u>retaining</u> staff at a CPA firm (check all that are most important):
   [ ] Firm reputation & prestige   [ ] Career growth opportunities
   [ ] Salary and benefits   [ ] Challenging projects
   [ ] Telecommuting & work from home options

3

Why it's so Great to Work at a CPA Firm
(Really, it is!)

A true story

At a wedding reception I attended a few years ago, as often happens I found myself seated at a table of eight people who didn't know each other. Gamely attempting conversation - to the extent it was possible over the loud music and din of 200 people having a gay old time - I introduced myself to the lady on my left. She was a friend of the groom's parents. She told me what she did for a living, and I told her about my work consulting with CPA firms.

"Wow," the lady said. "That's fascinating!"

I love what I do and feel that I'm good at it, but this was the first "Wow!" I'd ever gotten in response to a description of my life's calling. "Why so?" I asked her.

She back-pedaled a bit. "Well, I'm sure your work IS fascinating. But that's not why I was saying 'Wow.' You see, my son is a college sophomore. He just changed his major from English to accounting. His goal is to work at a CPA firm. I'm so thrilled! I don't know much about accounting, but I *do* know the job market for accountants is strong and that starting salaries are pretty high compared to most other undergraduate majors. I mean, what was he going to do with a B.A in English?"

Now I was thrilled too! Those of us in the accounting profession love to see young people selecting accounting as a major. For the last 20 years the popularity of accounting as a college major has dropped off precipitously. "Actually there's a <u>terrible</u> shortage of young staff at CPA firms across the country," I told her. "May I ask why your son changed his major to accounting?"

It was a familiar story. Her son had taken stock of himself and came to two realizations. First, he had always been good at math and loved working with figures. Second, he was somewhat introverted. The thought of sitting behind a desk all day pounding out the work and getting paid to do so was very appealing to him. "Accounting suits his personality," she said. "The lack of interaction with other people doesn't bother him. After all, he's not the most outgoing kid."

"I'm sorry to deflate your balloon, but your son has made a terrible mistake in choosing accounting as a career," I told her.

She smiled awkwardly and chuckled. "You're kidding, right?"

"Dead serious," I responded. "Mind you, I can only speak for accountants who work for CPA firms; that's the universe I know. Yes, we CPAs are perceived as dull, boring bean counters. We're not known for being people oriented. But that reputation is undeserved and wrongly stereotyped. It's something our profession hasn't been very effective at changing."

"You don't say," she answered, stifling a yawn.

The technical part of a CPA's job <u>is</u> important, I explained. Technical expertise is what everyone has to ante up to get in the game; if you can't master the technical skills, you'll soon find yourself out of a job.

"But the most effective CPAs spend the majority of their time interacting with people," I asserted. "If your son loves sitting at a desk all day crunching numbers, with no human contact, public accounting may not be the career for him.

"I'm not saying all CPAs are 'life of the party' types. But the most successful CPAs are those who interact well with other people and are seen by co-workers as being quite personable."

10

"This has been quite illuminating," the lady answered, turning quickly to strike up a conversation with the woman on her left.

Changing long held perceptions is difficult, but there's no doubt that CPAs spend most of their time interacting with people:

- **Co-workers.** When new hires first start working at CPA firms they are closely supervised by experienced CPAs and the firm's partners. Learning how to work with them as a member of a team takes place several hours a day, virtually every day.

  As young accountants gain experience, they begin to supervise younger staff. So, now the role reverses and the staff person must be effective as a trainer, supervisor and leader.

  Ultimately, to attain the pinnacle of achievement in a CPA firm – partnership - the staff person must gain the trust and confidence of the partner group, which requires strong interpersonal skills as well technical knowledge.

- **Clients.** Of all the groups of people that a CPA must establish effective relationships with, none is more important than client relationships. There is no question that clients value the work product prepared by their CPA. But there are dozens of other firms that can provide the same thing, probably just as proficiently. What clients *really* value is the quality of the *service* given to them, the CPA's responsiveness to their needs and the overall relationship that they develop with the team performing their work.

- **The community at-large.** Relationships between CPAs and attorneys, bankers, investment advisors, etc., are critically important. CPAs are on duty 24/7, always keeping their eyes peeled for new client opportunities in arenas such as their church or synagogue, civic and charitable organizations, the soccer field and golf course.

  Without these relationships, CPA firms would die on the vine because regardless of their technical prowess, they wouldn't have many clients to practice on.

11

The moral of this story is that a career at a CPA firm offers a wonderful opportunity to blend the use of the language of business – accounting –with exciting opportunities to work with the interesting and diverse personalities of co-workers, partners, clients and the many people that comprise the community at large.

What makes a career at a CPA firm so great?

Here are 12 reasons. Items with an asterisk were ranked highly in a recent survey by the AICPA/PCPS entitled "What Attracts and Retains Staff."

1. **Advancement opportunities.*** Most firms have at least four position levels that staff can be promoted to; some firms (generally, mid-sized and larger firms) have as many as eight. In addition to these job positions, staff advances <u>within</u> each position by getting assignments with progressively increasing amounts of responsibility and complexity.

2. **Interesting, challenging work.*** Solving clients' problems and meeting a wide variety of their needs is one of the most fascinating and rewarding aspects of a CPA's job. Each assignment is different from the next. Sure, there is some repetitive work that has to be done, but you would be hard-pressed to name any career that doesn't involve a certain amount of tedious work that one would prefer avoiding. Thankfully, the repetitive work drops sharply as you move up the ladder.

3. **Salary.*** A staff position in a CPA firm is one of the highest paying jobs that a college graduate can get without an advanced degree. This has been the case for 50 years or more. In Chicago, most firms pay new college graduates a starting salary of $55,000-$60,000 (includes bonus and overtime) for their first year. Jobs in the I.T. engineering and certain science areas may pay as much or slightly more than accounting degrees, but the vast majority of jobs pay substantially less.

Surveys indicating the younger generation values work-life balance over money have garnered a lot of press in the past 10 years. These findings have been erroneously interpreted by many as meaning that young people don't care about making money. This couldn't be further from the truth. Sure, young people want work-life balance. But survey after survey for the last 10 years shows that they want _money_, too!

4. **There will always be job opportunities at CPA firms.** CPA firms are pretty much recession-proof. Clients need their audits, accounting, tax and consulting work, regardless of the state of the economy. This was evidenced during the great recession of 2008-2011 when the CPA firm industry was able to stay flat while most industries witnessed sharp revenue _declines._ Most industries would have given their eye teeth to "just" stay even. Unfortunately, there were layoffs at CPA firms during the recession (the first time since the early 1990s), but they paled in comparison to most industries. And because most of the layoffs were from large firms, smaller firms hired laid-off personnel in droves.

5. **Access to cutting edge technology.*** As much as any other profession, CPAs' work has been heavily impacted by technology. The way CPAs do their jobs today is totally dependent on computers and completely different from the way things were done 20 or so years ago. Literally every aspect of a CPA's work has been successfully integrated with highly efficient technology. In many cases, technology has reduced the time spent in some of the more boring and tedious parts of the CPA's work.

6. **Constant training.** Every person in a CPA firm, from new college graduates through the most senior partners, receives formal training every year. The profession requires it. Personnel at most firms receive well in excess of the statutory requirement of 40 hours per year of annual training. The training is not just in accounting and tax, but computers and soft skills.

And here's the best part. Beyond the classroom training, young staff at firms receive rigorous on-the-job training. They actually get paid while they work and get trained at the same time! It's hard to imagine any other professional job that values training as much as CPAs.

7. **Baptism to the business world.** When students complete their accounting degrees, virtually all of their education to that point has been in accounting, business subjects and courses in liberal arts. Once college graduates begin working at CPA firms, they get a marvelous education to the business world. They are exposed to a wide variety of businesses and are in a great position to observe how they work, how they are organized, how they generate profits and how decisions are made. All while doing their accounting work!

8. **Comfortable office atmosphere.*** I have conducted a number of focus groups of new staff at CPA firms and asked them a host of questions regarding their jobs and the firms they work at. When asked what the best part of their job is, the most common response by far has been the "great work atmosphere and the people they work with." Drilling down on these responses, we received comments like "it's a joy that people are respectful of one another," "partners have so much fun," "people genuinely are interested in our success."

9. **A great career for women raising a family due to flexible scheduling options.*** Most CPA firms are as flexible as anyone could possibly imagine to accommodate women raising a family. One would be hard pressed to find any firm of substance without several flex-time (examples: a work schedule in which someone works 3 days a week or works until 3pm five days a week) women, including partners. A great deal of a CPA's work lends itself to working remotely from home and today's technology easily accommodates this. Clients have also shown themselves to be remarkably sensitive and understanding of CPA firm personnel working a flex-time schedule.

10. **The CPA firm industry is innovative.** Compared to all other professions, CPA firms are as innovative as any. Here are just a few examples:

- Use of cutting edge technology.
- Attention to soft skills training.
- University-like, curriculum-based training.
- Expansion of services well beyond accounting & tax to provide "one-stop shopping" for clients.
- Adoption of selling and marketing programs after decades of inactivity in these areas.
- Specialization.
- International issues.

11. **Team orientation to the work.** CPA firms have learned that clients are served more effectively when served by teams of professionals instead of individuals. The team orientation is also helpful to firms in the event that a key service provider suddenly leaves the firm because there is always back-up. Finally, staff enjoy working as part of a team because that's the way they have been learning throughout their years of formal education.

12. **Regular performance reviews.** The vast majority of firms provide performance reviews for all staff no less than annually. This is often combined with a formal mentoring program. Added bonus: Unless there is a terrible recession, staff can count on a salary increase at least once a year.

Partners love their jobs

You can tell a lot about the quality and job opportunities of a company by looking at its leaders, which for CPA firms, is, of course, the partners. I've consulted to CPA firms for over 20 years. During that time, I've consistently observed this about partners in CPA firms: They love their job! There's quite a lot of evidence for this observation:

- The vast majority of partners don't want to retire.
- Many don't want to merge into a larger firm and lose their identity.
- Most are willing to work long hours if that's what it takes to service their clients.
- They remain in their jobs despite the frustrations of serving clients with a severe shortage of labor.
- They are willing to forgo a substantial amount of additional income to invest heavily in marketing programs, technology and training.

It's not hard to see why they really love their jobs:

1. They love their clients.
2. They love their work and its challenges.
3. They love solving problems and saving the day for their clients.
4. They love the freedom and flexibility of being a business owner.
5. And they love making more money than they ever dreamed of – partners in local firms earn, on average, roughly $350,000-$400,000 a year.

4

Facts About
The CPA Profession

What do CPA firms do?

CPA firms typically provide three main types of services, with each service having several subgroups.

The mix of these three main services is shown on the next page, broken down by three sizes of firms:

- Big 4
- Large regional firms
- Local firms

Primary Services Provided by CPA Firms

		Big 4 (1)	Large Regionals (2)	Local Firms (3)
1.	Audit and accounting:			
	a. Audits	36%	32%	18%
	b. Reviews	4%	3%	2%
	c. Compilations, bkpg, payroll, etc.	1%	10%	20%
	TOTAL A&A	**41%**	**45%**	**40%**
2.	Tax:			
	a. Corporate/business	24%	27%	24%
	b. Individual/1040s	3%	9%	19%
	TOTAL TAX	**27%**	**36%**	**43%**
3.	Consulting (4):			
	a. Specific areas (4)	28%	14%	5%
	b. Handholding, misc. (5)	4%	5%	12%
	TOTAL CONSULTING	**32%**	**19%**	**17%**

(1) Accounting Today, Top 100 Firms in 2012

(2) IPA National Benchmarking Report

(3) The Rosenberg MAP Survey

(4) See the next page for a list of the most common types of consulting.

(5) The term "handholding" is used to describe arguably the most important work that CPAs do for their clients, even more important than accounting or tax, though the handholding could be related to A&A or tax issues. Generally, handholding occurs when the CPA and his/her client discuss and brainstorm ideas, opportunities, problems, challenges, alternative decisions, strategies and anything else that the key people in a business have on their minds. Specific examples include whether to buy or lease, hiring decisions, whether or not to purchase a business or a machine, how to plan for college, etc.

The Most Common Consulting Services and Niche Practice Areas

Percentages are derived from the number of non-Big 4 firms offering these services. Data is from the 2012 IPA National Benchmarking Report and the 2012 Accounting Today Top 100 Survey. Since both surveys report on firms predominantly in the Top 100, the percentages below are substantially different than those of the typical local firm.

Consulting

Estate and financial planning-78%
Employee benefits-73%
Business valuations – 68%
Litigation support – 63%
Forensic services – 49%
Investment advisory – 43%
Computer/IT – 41%
SOX compliance – 31%

Niche practice areas

Not for profit – 83%
Construction – 75%
Real estate – 72%
Wholesale/distribution – 60%
Health care – 56%
Law firms – 53%
Medical services – 51%
Governmental – 48%
Retail – 45%
High tech – 39%
Financial institutions/banking – 35%

Data on supply and demand for accounting graduates

Data below is from the AICPA's 2011 Survey of Trends in the Supply & Demand of Accounting Graduates and the Demand for Public Accounting Recruits. Results from 160 universities and 348 CPA firms.

Number of Students Enrolled in Degreed Accounting Programs

	Accounting Enrollment Undergrad + Grad	
1994-95	192,870	
2001-02	154,510	Down 20% from 1995
2006-07	203,368	
2007-08	212,834	
2009-10	226,108	Up 46% since 2001-02 or 6% per year during this 8 year period

New Accounting Grads Hired by CPA Firms

	Bachelor's Only	Bachelor's + Masters
1992	11,970	14,180
1989	25,240	27,840
1996	17,820	20,470
2002	12,630	15,295
2007	28,025	36,112
2010	19,870	33,321

Gender Breakdown of Graduates*

	Male %	Female %
1992	54%	46%
1996	49%	51%
2002	43%	57%
2010	52%	48%

*Per Rosenberg Survey, typical local CPA firm staff is 42% male & 58% female.

Common Position Titles at CPA Firms

	Titles most common at local firms	Some firms also have these positions
Entry level – staff assistant	Recent accounting graduate.	
Staff	Most firms don't have separate titles for these first two positions.	Completion of first year, but not yet a senior; little supervision of other staff.
Senior	<ul><li>First major promotion.</li><li>A senior performs most of the detailed work on a job.</li><li>Works one job at a time.</li><li>Begins to supervise other staff.</li><li>Lots of contact with partners.</li></ul>	
Super-visor		Intermediate promotion from senior but still below manager.
Manager	<ul><li>On track to be a partner **or** it's a permanent position for highly experienced staff.</li><li>Common to work on several jobs at the same time.</li><li>Heavy supervision of staff.</li><li>Lots of contact with partner.</li></ul>	
Senior Manager		Promotion from manager but still below partner.
Non-equity partner		<ul><li>Has most of the skills to become an equity partner.</li><li>Often a partner in training. Heavy relationship duties.</li><li>No one knows who is equity vs. non-equity ptr.</li><li>Is not an owner of the firm.</li></ul>
Equity (or full) partner	Highest position in the firm. An owner. Final responsibility for all client matters.	

The U.S. CPA firm market

There are roughly 45,000 CPA firms in the United States. The market is skewed significantly from large to small:

- The "Big 4" international firms (Ernst & Young, KPMG, PricewaterhouseCoopers and Deloitte) account for 36% of the industry's total revenue.

- There is a huge fall-off from the Big 4 to the next tier of firms: The smallest Big 4 firm is 5 times the size of the fifth biggest firm.

- The 200 largest firms account for 51% of the industry's total revenue.

- 41,000 of the 45,000 firms are very small companies; the vast majority employs well under ten total people.

- 30,000 of the 45,000 firms are sole practitioners.

The 45,000 firms are summarized in the chart on the next page.

U.S. CPA Firm Market Demographics

	Number Of Firms	Total Market Size (Billions)		Average Annual Revenues (Millions)	Range of Annual Revenues
		Dollars	Pct.		
The Big 4*	4	$32	36%	$8,000	$5B-11B
#5 to #50	46	10	11%	220	$60M-1B
#51 to #100	50	2	2%	40	$31M-57M
#101-#200	100	2	2%	20	$15M-30M
SUBTOTAL	200	46	51%		
Next 4,000	4,000	24	27%	6.0	$3M-15M
Very small multi-partner firms	11,000	14	15%	1.3	
Sole practitioners	30,000	6	7%	0.2	
Grand Total	45,000	$90	100%		

* The Big 4 are:
- Ernst & Young
- KPMG
- PricewaterhouseCoopers
- Deloitte

All data is approximated based on various sources of data and the author's knowledge of the industry.

Annual growth for North American Accounting Firms

The Enron scandal and Andersen collapse of 2001 were cataclysmic events in the history of our profession, resulting in five overarching developments that had enormous impact on virtually every multi-partner firm in the country from 2002 until the onset of the recession in the 4th quarter of 2008.

1. **Accounting scandals.** In 2000 and 2001, major corporate and accounting scandals occurred at companies such as Enron, Tyco International, Adelphia, Peregrine Systems and WorldCom. These scandals cost investors billions of dollars when the share prices of affected companies collapsed, shaking public confidence in the nation's securities markets.

2. **Creation of the Sarbanes-Oxley Act and PCAOB.** Congress reacted to these scandals by passing The Sarbanes-Oxley Act (affectionately known as SOX), which set new and enhanced standards for all U.S. public company boards, management and accounting firms. SOX created the Public Company Accounting Oversight Board (PCAOB) to oversee the auditors of public companies. One of the PCAOB's major duties is to enforce Section 404(b) of the Act, which requires a publicly-held company's auditor to attest to and report on management's assessment of its internal controls.

3. **Birth of new multi-billion revenue source for CPA firms: Section 404 work.** These requirements fueled the strongest revenue growth in the history of the CPA profession, primarily during what was referred to as "The Golden Age" – 2002 to 2007/08, the onset of the recession. A new billion dollar revenue source, referred to as "SOX work" or "Section 404 work", was created primarily for the national and larger regional CPA firms.

4. **Trickle-down effect.** This highly profitable work was so substantial that it caused the 20 or so largest firms in the country to focus heavily on their public company practices and neglect their smaller clients, enabling the next tier of firms – regional and large locals – to pick up the near-abandoned clients of the

24

nationals. This, in turn, created great opportunities for the next smaller group of firms, and so on, in what has been referred to as a "trickle down" effect.

5. **Creation of a Perfect Storm for CPA firms.** This new billion dollar revenue source for the national and large regional firms created a huge hiring demand at national and large regional firms, luring staff that might have joined local firms. This resulted in the tightest labor market for CPA firm staff in the history of the profession. Hiring of experienced staff by local firms became nearly impossible.

But wait. It gets worse. Section 404 work, lucrative to the CPA firms, proved to be incredibly boring work for the staff, requiring long overtime hours outside of the tax season and heavy travel for some. It burned out thousands of young staffers on the CPA profession, shattering the typical decades-long migration of young people from national to local firms after they obtained top-notch training from the large firms. These people simply had enough of working for a CPA firm and sought their next job outside of public accounting, thereby shrinking the labor pool even further.

This created a "Perfect Storm" for CPA firms during the Golden Age: Record high demand for services and record low supply of staff.

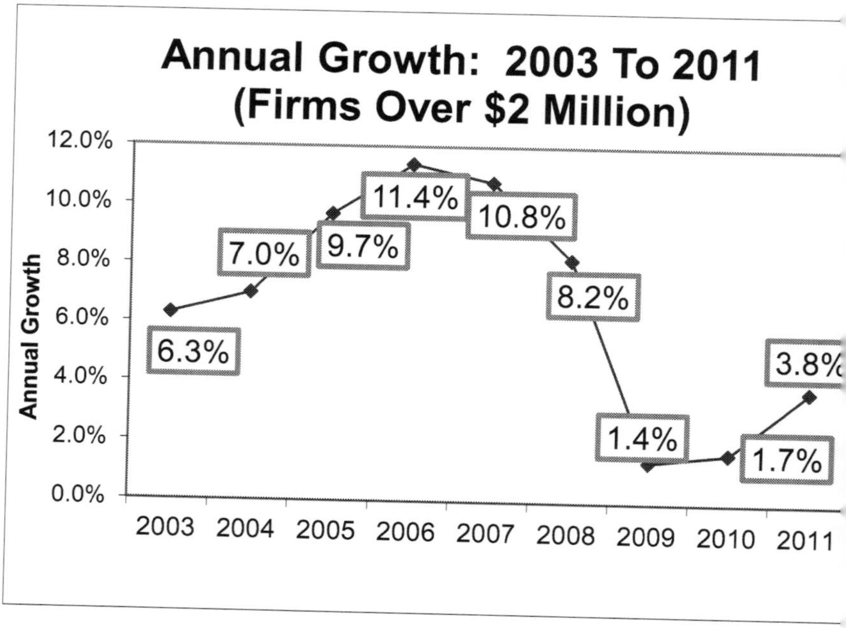
Annual Growth: 2003 To 2011
(Firms Over $2 Million)
Annual Growth
12.0%
10.0%
8.0%
6.0%
4.0%
2.0%
0.0%
6.3%
7.0%
9.7%
11.4%
10.8%
8.2%
1.4%
1.7%
3.8%
2003
2004
2005
2006
2007
2008
2009
2010
2011

<u>The changing landscape of the Top 20 firms in the U.S.</u>

The 4 key trends in the CPA industry today are:

1. Dire shortage of labor.
2. Baby Boomer partners retiring in droves.
3. The two trends above creating a succession planning crisis.
4. Merger mania.

We'll be examining all major trends in the CPA firm industry, but for now let's look at the changes at the largest 20 firms in the U.S. that resulted from the many mergers of the last 20 years:

Top 20 Firms in the U.S.
1993 vs. 2012

1993 (Public Accounting Report)

		U.S. Revenue ($Millions)
1.	Arthur Andersen **(gone)**	2,680
2.	Ernst & Young	2,281
3.	Deloitte & Touche	1,955
4.	KPMG	1,800
5.	Coopers & Lybrand **(gone)**	1,557
6.	Price Waterhouse	1,370
7.	Grant Thornton	222
8.	McGladrey & Pullen	197
9.	Kenneth Leventhal **(gone)**	188
10.	BDO Seidman	182
11.	BKD	59
12.	Crowe Chizek	58
13.	Clifton Gunderson **(gone)**	50
14.	Plante Moran	49
15.	Moss Adams	47
16.	Altschuler Melvoin **(gone)**	42
17.	Geo S. Olive **(gone)**	38
18.	Richard Eisner	30
19.	Goldstein Golub **(gone)**	29
20.	FERS **(gone)**	25

2012 Accounting Today

		U.S. Revenue ($Millions)
1.	Deloitte	11,939
2.	PwC	8,844
3.	Ernst & Young	7,500
4.	KPMG	5,361
5.	McGladrey & Pullen	1,370
6.	Grant Thornton	1,146
7.	CBIZ **(new)**	598
8.	BDO	572
9.	Crowe Horwath	530
10.	BKD	391
11.	Moss Adams	323
12.	Plante Moran	304
13.	Dixon Hughes **(new)**	295
14.	Larson Allen **(new)**	285
15.	Marcum **(new)**	274
16.	Eisner Amper	255
17.	J.H. Cohn **(new)**	243
18.	Baker Tilly **(new)**	242
19.	Reznick **(new)**	203
20.	UHY **(new)**	186

27

Noteworthy observations about the Top 20 list:

- Eight of the Top 20 firms in 1993 no longer exist in 2013. Seven of the firms merged out of existence; Arthur Andersen famously collapsed.

- The revenue of the #1 firm in 2012 is 4.5 times greater than the revenue of 1993's #1 firm.

- The revenue of the 20th largest firm in 2012 is 7.4 times greater than the 20th largest in 1993.

- The large regionals have begun a slow but steady invasion of the hallowed turf of the Big 4 (6): In 1993, the smallest firm in the Big 6 was 6.2 times the size of the next biggest firm. In 2013, the smallest Big 4 firm is only 3.9 times the next largest firm.

Clearly mergers are fueling faster paced growth at the large regionals than at the Big 4 (6) firms. What is triggering these mergers? These are the primary causes:

1. Succession planning, primarily the aging of the partners coupled with a lack of younger partners to buy them out.

2. Lack of leadership at smaller firms.

3. Synergies that enable the combined firm to better meet their clients' needs with a more diverse portfolio of services and broader geographic coverage:

   - Both firms share similar specialties.
   - One firm is looking for a specialty that the other has developed.
   - One firm is strong in a geographic market that is sought by the other.
   - One firm is stronger in a particular service than the other. The result will be a greater ability to serve clients due to the increased diversity.

4. Bigger is better. Larger firms (measured by revenues) are almost always more profitable than smaller firms because the combined resources of the two firms attain a "critical mass" that enables them to be more effective at marketing, training, recruiting, technology and administration.

5. Recruiting becomes easier (not easy). When firms merge to form a larger firm, the combined firm is viewed more attractively to recruits.

6. Mergers can be a more economical way to acquire market share than trying to do it organically.

7. The drive for profitability. Merging in smaller firms is a great way to increase profitability.

5

CPA Firm Economics 101

The economic structure of a CPA firm

One of the main purposes of this monograph is to provide CPA firm personnel with an understanding of how their firm makes money and what holds back profitability. With this knowledge, team members will make better decisions about how they spend their time and perform their work.

All businesses have economic structures unique to their industries:

- Grocery stores are high volume, low profit margin.
- Real estate ventures use accelerated depreciation and other tax "angles" to generate cash flow.
- Professional sports teams focus on increasing the value of the franchise so it can eventually be sold for a gigantic profit.

The typical CPA firm is a **low volume, high priced business**, with a relatively high profit margin (generally 30-45% of revenue). This results from two factors:

- The supply of CPAs and CPA firms is relatively low compared to many professions. There is competition, but established firms don't worry too much about competing firms.

There are several formidable barriers to entry: the work is technically demanding and growing in complexity. While not rocket science, accounting requires a high level of intelligence and aptitude that many people don't possess. It's also very hard to attract clients, especially if you start from scratch without an established client base.

- The supply of labor is extremely low. Accounting is not considered "exciting" or popular by many young people. As a result, one of the principal operating tactics of CPA firms is allocating their scarce labor resources to those clients and projects that generate the most revenues.

The vast majority of a CPA firm's revenues is considered "annuity" business. Clients of CPA firms typically remain with their firms for 5-10 years or more, thereby providing a relatively "safe" revenue stream that continues every year, primarily compliance projects such as audits, reviews, compilations, bookkeeping and tax returns.

Most expenses are fixed vs. variable: Even though staff labor is theoretically a variable cost, with the exception of major recessions, the headcount at firms stays relatively constant despite fluctuations in revenue. Most firms can absorb a certain number of new clients without increasing their personnel headcount.

Also, due to the extreme shortage of labor, most CPA firms are continuously in a hiring mode: if a firm is fortunate enough to come across someone who has a good resume and is available, the person will generally be hired immediately, even though the firm's revenue volume might not appear to justify increasing headcount.

Low overhead expenses. CPA firms have low overheads compared to law firms and other businesses. Despite earning substantial profits, the vast majority of CPA firms are not big spenders. Many have very nice offices but would never be considered lavish. A very small percentage of a CPA firm's expenses are discretionary.

CPA firms are "top line" driven. In the pursuit of increased profitability, many businesses are presented with two alternatives: Increase revenues or decrease expenses. But CPA firms rarely focus on controlling expenses because there is little excess to trim. Instead, virtually all of the focus is on generating increased revenues. This is done by:

- Bringing in new business and clients.
- Increasing billing rates.
- Increasing realization - billing a higher percentage of time spent on client work.
- Increasing productivity – getting personnel to bill more hours and work more efficiently.

As a result of the above, CPA firms are considered "top line driven" businesses: Increases in revenue drop directly to the bottom line (profits) because these revenue increases rarely cause the firm's expenses to rise very much.

Leverage is king. The vast majority of the work performed by a CPA firm can be done by staff instead of partners. Therefore, one of the top operating strategies of firms is to maximize the amount of client work that each partner can create for non-partners to perform, under their supervision. Achieving this high leverage frees up partners' time to devote to practice development, nurturing relationships with clients and referral sources and helping staff learn and grow.

Bigger is better. Any analysis of CPA firm profitability will consistently and conclusively show that the higher a firm's revenues, the higher their profits will be. This is because the bigger the firm, the more affordably it can engage in sophisticated marketing programs, develop specialties and niches, aggressively pursue mergers, create better training programs and hire high level professionals in the administrative, marketing, HR and IT areas. All of these tactics attract larger clients (who pay higher fees), more talented staff and smaller firms looking to merge in.

33

Why should employees care how the firm makes money?

The cynics among you might ask this question. After all, the profits that the firm earns from the staff's great work goes directly into the partner's pockets, right?

The answer lies in the following axiom:

A highly profitable firm produces many tangible professional benefits for firm personnel.

What incentive do staff have to contribute to firm profitability? What's in it for them? Here are four good reasons:

1. Some of the profits flow directly to the staff in the form of higher salaries and bonuses. High levels of compensation enable the firm to retain its best people.

2. More money is available for career-enhancing training programs, updated technology, top notch marketing and other niceties such as modern (not lavish) offices.

3. Capital is available to merge in smaller firms and attract larger and more sophisticated clients, creating new client opportunities for the staff.

4. When a company's revenues and profits are increasing, a funny thing happens to office morale: everyone is happier! Firm personnel are more fun to be with, more helpful and more willing to work together. Bosses are more patient and smile more often.

The opposite of all those things happen when companies struggle. Ask anyone who has had the misfortune of working for a stagnant organization that struggles with profitability. It can be miserable.

Key definitions

Charge hours or billable hours. A CPA firm's widgets are their hours (apologies to Ron Baker). The vast majority of a firm's revenue is billed directly or indirectly by the hour, so CPA firms pay a lot of attention to the billable hours worked by their personnel.

Non-charge or non-billable hours. All time that is <u>not</u> worked on client projects. This includes training, firm meetings, practice development, vacation, holiday and sick time.

Billing rate. All personnel, from partner to staff, are assigned standard hourly billing rates. At some firms, personnel may have different billing rates for different types of work (i.e., audit vs. tax). These rates, when multiplied by the hours worked on client work, results in a number called **"gross fees" or "billable time."**

Timesheet. All charge and non-charge hours are recorded on timesheets. These charge hours are entered into the firm's billing system and accumulate in the firm's work-in-process , which is the starting point for generating client invoices.

Work-in-Process (WIP). A "receptacle" in the time and billing system where all time and out-of-pocket expenses are accumulated by client. When clients are billed part or all of the accumulated WIP, these billings are deducted from WIP balances, leaving a net unbilled amount for each client. These amounts are either carried forward to subsequent months to be billed at a later date or written off.

Write-offs. CPA firms (law firms, too) are rarely able to bill for 100% of their actual time spent on client work. The value of client work that is not billed to clients is called "write-offs." The vast majority of firms write off 10-20% of their client time.

There are many reasons for the write-offs, some of which are:

- Project inefficiencies that cannot be passed on to clients.
- Discounts given to clients to procure the engagement.
- Experienced personnel often use client engagements to teach less experienced staff how to perform their work. This is known as "on the job training" and often, cannot be billed to clients.

Realization percentage. Percentage of all client work that is billed to clients. The realization for most CPA firms is in the 80-90% range.

Billings are the actual amount of fees that are invoiced to clients. The difference between gross fees (the value of all time worked on client projects) and billings (sometimes called net fees or net revenues) is write-offs.

Leverage. This is a term used in many industries and it has a different meaning in each of them. In CPA firms, there are two interrelated ways to define leverage:

- A partner delegating client work to a staff person. The more staff that each partner can keep busy with client work, the more the firm is considered "leveraged."

- Leverage is measured as follows: If a firm has 5 partners and 25 professional staff (administrative staff are not included in this computation), the staff-partner ratio is 5:1. Staff-partner ratio is a principle way that CPA firms measure leverage.

Income per partner. The total earnings of all partners divided by the total number of partners. IPP is the primary measure of a CPA firm's profitability.

The 4 most important metrics used to manage CPA firm profits

The following 4 metrics are key to any analysis of CPA firm profitability.

1. **Fees per partner**. The firm's billings divided by the number of partners. This is one of the ways we measure leverage. The more billings each partner can manage, the higher the firm's profit margin. On average, partners work 10-15% of all work performed for clients; the remaining 85-90% is performed by staff under the partners' supervision. The higher the percentage of all client work performed by the partners, the harder it is for them to find the time to build their client base and help the firm achieve a high fees-per-partner ratio. So, in order to properly manage a large client base, partners need to delegate as much of the client work as possible to staff.

2. **Fees per person**. This is another leverage metric. The "person" part of the calculation is every employee in the firm, including administrative people. Firm headcount is measured in full time equivalents or FTEs. Someone who works 1,000 hours a year would be considered a 0.5 FTE. One who works 1,200 hours a year would be a 0.6 FTE. No one can ever be more than a 1.0 FTE, regardless of how many overtime hours they work.

3. **Staff to partner ratio** – The third leverage metric. It is the number of professional staff (all client service staff that are not equity partners) divided by the number of equity partners.

4. **Billing rates**. The rates assigned to each person in the firm that are used to multiply by charge hours to arrive at billings.

Many years ago, a great managing partner told me that the key to CPA firm profitability is "leverage and rates," epitomized by the four metrics above.

What CPA firm income statements look like

The typical CPA firm income statement looks something like this:

	Amount	Percent of Net Fees
Gross fees	$5,000,000	
Write-offs	500,000	
Net fees or billings	4,500,000	100.0%
Expenses:		
Staff salaries and benefits	2,000,000	44.4%
Overhead expenses*	1,000,000	22.2%
Total expenses	3,000,000	66.6%
Total income to the partners	$1,500,000	33.4%

* Rent, office supplies, marketing, insurance, training, IT costs, etc.

Illustrations of CPA firm profitability

The spreadsheets on the next six pages illustrate the income statement of a mythical CPA firm that is grossly under-performing, and how it changes as practices are initiated to improve the firm.

Grayed areas represent changes from the previous spreadsheet.

The six exhibits are summarized below.

	Spreadsheet Model	Result
A	Basic starting model.	A very weak firm.
B	Increase leverage-move work from partners to staff. Also, Partner A becomes MP and reduces his billable hours substantially to free up time to manage the firm.	Initially, the firm's profits go down because work formally billed at partner rates are now billed at staff rates.
C	Increase realization from 75% to 85% by more aggressive pricing and reducing write-offs with better supervision.	Income per partner (IPP) increases from 153,000 to 219,000.
D	Increase outlay for marketing as the firm's first step to generating higher revenues.	IPP goes down a tad due to the up-front outlay for marketing.
E	Increase billing rates – get them to at least *equal* the competition.	IPP goes up dramatically, from 204,000 to 304,000.
F	Revenues increase at a healthy clip because of the firm's marketing plan and the partners being freed up for practice development.	

ABC CPA Firm   **Exhibit A**

Base Firm

	FTE	Charge Hours	Billing Rate	Billable Fees
Partner A	1	1,800	225	405,000
Partner B	1	1,700	225	382,500
Partner C	1	1,700	225	382,500
Partner D	1	1,700	225	382,500
Managers	2	1,300	150	390,000
Seniors	4	1,300	110	572,000
Staff	3	1,300	90	351,000
Admin	3			
	16	18,600		
Gross Fees				2,865,500
Realization				75.0%
NET FEES(BILLINGS)				2,149,125

NET FEES(BILLINGS)	2,149,125	100.0%

EXPENSES:

Salaries	767,000	35.7%
Benefits	115,050	5.4%
Marketing	10,746	0.5%
Other	475,000	22.1%
Total expenses	1,367,796	63.6%
PARTNER PROFIT	781,329	36.4%

METRICS	ACTUAL	NORM
Fees per partner	537,281	1,071,000
Fees per person	134,320	165,000
Staff-partner ratio	2.3	4.6
Charge hours-partners	1,725	1,131
Charge hours-staff	1,300	1,502
Income per partner	195,332	345,000

ABC CPA Firm   **Exhibit B**

Move work from partners to staff. Also, Partner A becomes MP.

	FTE	Charge Hours	Billing Rate	Billable Fees
Partner A	1	800	225	180,000
Partner B	1	1,400	225	315,000
Partner C	1	1,400	225	315,000
Partner D	1	1,400	225	315,000
Managers	2	1,425	150	427,500
Seniors	4	1,550	110	682,000
Staff	3	1,500	90	405,000
Admin	3			
	16	18,550		

Gross Fees	2,639,500	
Realization	75.0%	
NET FEES(BILLINGS)	1,979,625	100.0%
EXPENSES:		
Salaries	767,000	38.7%
Benefits	115,050	5.8%
Marketing	10,746	0.5%
Other	475,000	24.0%
Total expenses	1,367,796	69.1%
PARTNER PROFIT	611,829	30.9%

METRICS	ACTUAL	NORM
Fees per partner	494,906	1,071,000
Fees per person	123,727	165,000
Staff-partner ratio	2.3	4.6
Charge hours-partners	1,250	1,131
Charge hours-staff	1,506	1,502
Income per partner	152,957	345,000

41

ABC CPA Firm   Exhibit C
Increase realization from 75% to 85%

	FTE	Charge Hours	Billing Rate	Billable Fees
Partner A	1	800	225	180,000
Partner B	1	1,400	225	315,000
Partner C	1	1,400	225	315,000
Partner D	1	1,400	225	315,000
Managers	2	1,425	150	427,500
Seniors	4	1,550	110	682,000
Staff	3	1,500	90	405,000
Admin	3			
	16	18,550		

Gross Fees	2,639,500	
Realization	85.0%	
NET FEES(BILLINGS)	2,243,575	100.0%

EXPENSES:

Salaries	767,000	34.2%
Benefits	115,050	5.1%
Marketing	10,746	0.5%
Other	475,000	21.2%
Total expenses	1,367,796	61.0%
PARTNER PROFIT	875,779	39.0%

METRICS	ACTUAL	NORM
Fees per partner	560,894	1,071,000
Fees per person	140,223	165,000
Staff-partner ratio	2.3	4.6
Charge hours-partners	1,250	1,131
Charge hours-staff	1,506	1,502
Income per partner	218,945	345,000

ABC CPA Firm Exhibit D

Increase marketing- 1st step to generating higher revenues

	FTE	Charge Hours	Billing Rate	Billable Fees
Partner A	1	800	225	180,000
Partner B	1	1,400	225	315,000
Partner C	1	1,400	225	315,000
Partner D	1	1,400	225	315,000
Managers	2	1,425	150	427,500
Seniors	4	1,550	110	682,000
Staff	3	1,500	90	405,000
Admin	3			
	16	18,550		
Gross Fees				2,639,500
Realization				85.0%
NET FEES(BILLINGS)				2,243,575	100.0%

EXPENSES:

Salaries	767,000	34.2%
Benefits	115,050	5.1%
Marketing	70,000	3.1%
Other	475,000	21.2%
Total expenses	1,427,050	63.6%
PARTNER PROFIT	816,525	36.4%

METRICS	ACTUAL	NORM
Fees per partner	560,894	1,071,000
Fees per person	140,223	165,000
Staff-partner ratio	2.3	4.6
Charge hours-partners	1,250	1,131
Charge hours-staff	1,506	1,502
Income per partner	204,131	345,000

43

ABC CPA Firm **Exhibit E**
Increase Billing Rates

	FTE	Charge Hours	Billing Rate	Billable Fees	
Partner A	1	800	275	220,000	As rates go up, ptrs do less billable work that staff can do.
Partner B	1	1,250	275	343,750	
Partner C	1	1,250	275	343,750	
Partner D	1	1,250	275	343,750	
Managers	2	1,475	180	531,000	
Seniors	4	1,600	135	864,000	
Staff	3	1,550	100	465,000	
Admin	3				
	16	18,550			

Gross Fees	3,111,250	
Realization	85.0%	
NET FEES(BILLINGS)	2,644,563	100.0%
EXPENSES:		
Salaries	767,000	29.0%
Benefits	115,050	4.4%
Marketing	70,000	2.6%
Other	475,000	18.0%
Total expenses	1,427,050	54.0%
PARTNER PROFIT	1,217,513	46.0%

METRICS	ACTUAL	NORM
Fees per partner	661,141	1,071,000
Fees per person	165,285	165,000
Staff-partner ratio	2.3	4.6
Charge hours-partners	1,138	1,131
Charge hours-staff	1,556	1,502
Income per partner	304,378	345,000

44

ABC CPA Firm

More revenues generated and more staff hired to do additional work.

	FTE	Charge Hours	Billing Rate	Billable Fees	
Partner A	1	800	275	220,000	
Partner B	1	1,250	275	343,750	
Partner C	1	1,250	275	343,750	
Partner D	1	1,250	275	343,750	
Managers	3	1,475	180	796,500	
Seniors	9	1,600	135	1,944,000	
Staff	7	1,550	100	1,085,000	
Admin	6				
	29	34,225			
Gross Fees				5,076,750	
Realization				85.0%	
NET FEES(BILLINGS)				4,315,238	100.0%
EXPENSES:					
Salaries				1,546,333	35.8%
Benefits				231,950	5.4%
Marketing				112,196	2.6%
Other				863,048	20.0%
Total expenses				2,753,527	63.8%
PARTNER PROFIT				1,561,710	36.2%

METRICS	ACTUAL	NORM
Fees per partner	1,078,809	1,071,000
Fees per person	148,801	165,000
Staff-partner ratio	4.8	4.6
Charge hours-partners	1,138	1,131
Charge hours-staff	1,562	1,502
Income per partner	390,428	345,000

Billing and timesheet flowchart

The next page is a flowchart of a hypothetical client engagement. The process, from beginning to end, is as follows:

1. Obtain the client
2. Quote a fee of $2,100.
3. The partner budgets the job for $2,333, anticipating write-offs of 10% because it's a first year project.
4. The work is completed by the three-person team in one day. Each person accounts for a full eight hour day on his/her timesheets.
5. The three professionals work the job, amassing billable time of $2,760, which is $660 over the quoted fee of $2,100.
6. $660 is written off. The team worked more time on the project than the firm was able to bill.
7. The client is billed for $2,100.

How could the firm have averted the write-offs? Here are some possibilities:

1. The partner spends one hour on the job instead of three, delegating the other two hours to the staff.

2. Staff person B had 3 of his 6 hours written off, perhaps indicative of being poorly trained and supervised. With better supervision, perhaps the staff person would have spent 4 or 5 hours on the job instead of 6.

✳ 3. Perhaps some of the hours spent by the two staff was on work that either the client should have done or were on additional work requested by the client. In either event, if the staff would have notified the partner and the client of this, the extra hours might have been billed in addition to the $2,100.

✳ Staff need to understand engagement and managers need to communicate engagement objectives to staff.

46

BILLING & TIMESHEET FLOWCHART

Get Client/**Quote Fee** of $2,100

Budget set for $2,333 Assumes 90.0% Write-off

rtner Timesheet	
arge	Non-Charge
hrs	5 hrs

Staff A Timesheet	
Charge	Non-Charge
7 hrs	1 hr

Staff B T-Sheet	
Charge	NC
6 hrs	2 hrs

Work In Process

	Hours	Rate	Fees
Partner	3	300	900
Staff A	7	180	1260
Staff B	6	100	600
TOTAL	16		**2760**

Billing

	Hours	Rate	Fees
Partner	3	300	900
Staff A	5	180	900
Staff B	3	100	300
TOTAL			**2100**

Write-Offs

	Hours	Rate	Fees
Partner	0		
Staff A	2	180	360
Staff B	3	100	300
TOTAL			**660**

Billing for $2,100

Realization 76.1%

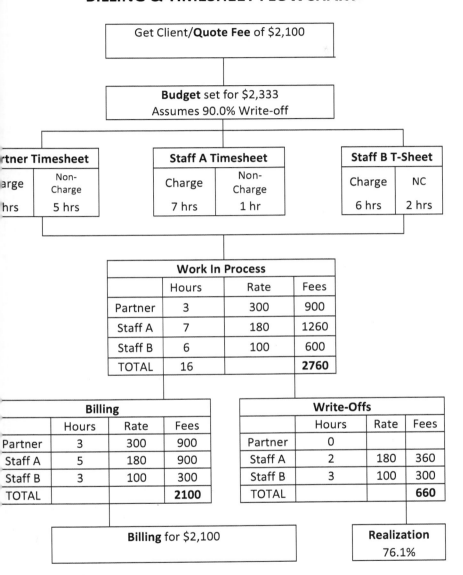

Examples of how various actions impact a CPA firm's profits

Assume a firm with 8 partners and 28 professional staff.

1. **Everyone in the firm records only one <u>extra</u> billable hour per week.** Notice I said "records," not "works" an extra hour. Both partners and staff perform hundreds, if not thousands of hours on client work that is recorded as non-billable time instead of billable time. Why? It could be sloppiness in keeping track of time. Or perhaps someone feels guilty about spending too much time on a task. Maybe a manager spends a couple of hours training a staff person on a client engagement and makes a unilateral judgment that the time shouldn't be billed to the client. In many cases, this extra time <u>can</u> be billed to the client. But if the time never makes it to the billings records, it will never be billed.

    - 1 hour x 48 weeks per year, x 36 people = 1,728 hours
    - @ blended billing rate of $130, additional revenue=$225,000
    - @90% realization, $203,000 of additional profits.

2. **Bringing in a $5,000 client.** Assume that half of the 36 client service personnel were able to bring in <u>one</u> $5,000 client per year.

    - 18 people x $5,000 each = $90,000 of new revenue.
    - At 35% incremental profit, that = $59,000 per year.

    If the client averages a ten year tenure with the firm, the present value at 5% per year is $300,000.

3. **Losing a $5,000 client.** The reverse of #2. If half of the client-service personnel in the firm provided such poor service to a client that they left the firm, the cost to the firm would be $300,000.

4. **Investing time in staff training**. Assume the effort is made by a managers and partners to spend more time training staff so that each staff person, on average, is able to bill one additional hour per week.

- 1 hour x 48 weeks x 28 staff x $100 per hour = $134,000.
- @ 90% realization = $121,000.
- If training time cost $25,000, incremental profit = $96,000.

5. **Partners push down work to staff and use the freed-up time to bring in new clients**. Assume the 8 partners delegate 100 billable hours each, per year, to staff. Further assume that the 800 hours of freed up time is used for practice development and that the result of those efforts is additional $400,000 of revenues.

If the partners' billing rate is $250 and the staff's blended rate is $110, that's a difference of $140 per hour. If 800 hours of work previously billed by partners is now billed by staff, the reduced revenue would be $112,000.

- New business $400,000
- Reduced partner hours   <u>112,000</u>
- Profit increase $288,000

It's important to note that the firm should not reduce billings to clients simply because work formerly done by partners is now being done by staff.

6. **Impact of poor staff productivity**. Assume that the firm's 28 staff averages a disappointingly low 1,400 billable hours per year. If the firm can improve their staff's productivity by increasing the average to 1,600 billable hours from 1,400, a very realistic goal, the firm could make do with 24 staff instead of 28.

- Saving the cost of four people at a cost of $80,000 each (includes benefits)= $320,000.

Benchmarking norms for CPA firms

The following is from The 2012 Rosenberg MAP Survey. Data is for 2011.

Annual Fees	Fees Per Partner	Fees Per Person	Staff Partner Ratio	Partner Billing Rate	Income Per Partner	Billable Hours PTRS	Billable Hours STAFF
2-10M							
-2011	1,059,491	160,278	4.5	272	333,567	1,113	1,492
-2010	1,074,086	158,415	4.7	269	332,228	1,117	1,475
-2009	1,042,199	150,973	4.7	263	325,523	1,142	1,471
10-20M							
-2011	1,415,693	171,787	5.6	318	406,174	1,108	1,516
-2010	1,436,163	168,165	5.8	313	418,043	1,090	1,494
-2009	1,319,323	161,551	5.6	308	402,592	1,099	1,483
>20M							
-2011	1,795,339	174,112	7.4	350	515,895	1,095	1,474
-2010	1,930,730	173,514	8.0	354	472,838	1,079	1,436
-2009	1,802,154	167,815	7.9	356	448,277	1,047	1,408

The main takeaway from this chart is that generally speaking, the larger the firm, the stronger the performance, especially in profits - as indicated by Income Per Partner.

6

How CPA Firms Get Clients

When students attend college and major in accounting, they are blissfully unaware of what will make them successful in a public accounting career. That's probably as it should be because the universities' main job is to provide the technical foundation in the accounting and business disciplines necessary to work in the business world.

Few experts in managing a CPA firm would disagree with this short list of key success factors:

1. Maintain a great staff, including recruiting, training, leadership development and mentoring.
2. Develop expertise and talent.
3. Provide quality service that totally satisfies clients' needs.
4. Provide quality work.
5. Maintain a healthy level of profitability.
6. Manage the firm effectively.

...and, the subject of this chapter...

7. ...Bring in business.

Many new hires are unaware of the importance of bringing in business. This naiveté is perpetuated at many CPA firms, particularly the smaller ones. The apocryphal story goes like this:

The managing partner summons a manager in the firm to his office to give her the good news that she has been selected as the next partner in the firm. He says: "Congratulations. Now go out there and bring in some business."

The manager's face registers shock. Never once in her ten years with the firm has bringing in business been discussed with her. Certainly, no one has given her any training in business development.

A few definitions before we proceed

Marketing. Activities that create name recognition and awareness of the firm in its markets. This includes branding, promotional materials, direct mail campaigns, putting on seminars, publishing a firm newsletter or blog and many other activities. It's a lot easier to sell professional services to a prospective client when that person is already familiar with your firm and views it in a positive light – that's the job of marketing.

Selling. Also called practice development or business development. Most CPA firms are reluctant to use the word "selling" due to its negative connotation to CPAs. Selling is the act of asking for the order, and getting it. Selling professional services (as opposed to selling a product) almost always requires the professional to establish a relationship with the client before, during and after the sale. A major part of the relationship development is identifying the clients' needs and showing how the firm can meet those needs.

3 categories of business-getters:

- **Rainmakers.** Someone who is highly effective at bringing in substantial volumes of business, year after year. Often times, the rainmaker's personality more closely resembles that of a traditional sales person than the stereotypic accountant. Rainmakers are not very common in CPA firms, especially at smaller firms. Well under 10% of all partners are true rainmakers.

- **Effective business-getters.** Clearly below the rainmaker, but very active in his/her practice development efforts and enjoys a steady amount of success most years in bringing in a respectable volume of business. No more than 20% of all partners are effective business-getters.

- **Mist makers.** Firm personnel, both partners and staff, who make small but noteworthy contributions to the firm's business-getting efforts. Many firms feel that it's preferable to have a firm of many mist makers instead of relying on one or two rainmakers.

Referral sources. Outside professionals that recommend your firm to a prospective client. The most common referral sources are lawyers, bankers, money managers, insurance salesmen, employee benefit and retirement consultants. Cultivating win-win relationships with referral sources is a critically important aspect of practice development.

Some professionals form referral relationships on a *quid pro quo* basis: If they give out a referral, they expect one in return. Others, while they prefer reciprocal referral relationships, are reasonably content making one-way referrals because their top priority is to help *their* client.

Cold calling. Initiating contact with a prospect or referral source that you have never met. The communication can be a telephone call, email or letter. The vast majority of firms do not make cold calls because they are widely considered ineffective and CPAs generally hate making them.

New clients don't hang from trees

None of the seven success factors listed on the first page of this chapter are "easy" to do well. But of all seven, bringing in business wins the award for the *most* critical function that CPAs are the *least* effective at doing. The majority dislike practice development and aren't very good at it. The common refrain from partners is: "I didn't go to college to get an accounting degree to become a salesman."

There are those who feel that people who pursue accounting careers are introverts who tend not to possess the personality necessary to sell effectively. This sweeping generalization has some truth to it, but there are many exceptions.

Nonetheless, the reality is that unless *someone* brings in business, the firm will eventually die out.

The chart on the next page lists several reasons why CPA firms need to continuously bring in new clients.

WHY CPA FIRMS NEED TO GROW

1. **Need to bring in new business just to stay even.** 10-20% of client projects from the prior year don't repeat. This is due primarily to clients leaving the firm, clients merging out of existence and one-time projects such as client mergers, IRS audits or estate plans, that don't repeat the following year. So this means that in order for a CPA firm to just *maintain* the same revenue volume from the previous year, it has to bring in 10-20% new business.

2. **Best way to grow the bottom line is to grow the top line.** The quickest path to increased profitability is to generate more revenues because the profits drop directly to the bottom line. Why? The cost structure of a CPA firm is largely fixed vs. variable. Most firms can absorb a fair amount of additional work without hiring more people or incurring additional overhead expenses.

3. **Advancement opportunities for your people.** Growth provides new opportunities for your staff. It's exciting to be assigned to a new client and staff view the increased challenge as a very positive experience. Quality staff rarely stay at a stagnant firm.

4. **Priming the pump.** A fundamental concept of selling professional services is that practice development cannot be easily turned on if you have been inactive at it for a period of time. Selling needs to be done on a continual basis to be effective.

5. **Growth energizes the firm.** People like working for firms that are "going places." When staff see the firm continuously bringing in new clients, that's impressive. It makes them feel that the firm has such a strong reputation in the community.

6. **Monkey sees, monkey does.** If you want your staff to develop a good attitude towards practice development, it has to start with the partners. If the partners aren't selling, the staff reason: "If the partners don't do it, why should I?"

How firms get clients: The Marketing Funnel

It's hard to believe, but until 1978, CPA and law firms were ethically prohibited from soliciting prospective clients for their business. Since this change, the tactics used by CPAs to market their firms has evolved substantially, though the stagnation at some firms makes it seem as though they have yet to hear the news.

The funnel is a geometric figure that is wider at the top, tapering down until it is quite narrow at the bottom. The funnel is very useful in illustrating three integrated techniques that CPA firms employ to market their services. Each layer of the funnel paves the way for the layer below it. The marketing funnel is illustrated on the next page.

Broadcast phase. The top layer of the funnel is called the broadcast phase. The funnel is at its widest at the top, paralleling the purpose of broadcast activities – to reach the widest possible audience with messages that create name recognition and brand awareness. Like a good lead-off man in baseball, the broadcast phase "sets the table" for the next phase, the networking phase. In the broadcast phase, communication is one way – from the firm to the target audience – and is not intended to generate sales.

Networking phase. After the firm has done a good job of creating name recognition, firm partners and staff can begin targeting its audience with a variety of networking activities. Networking activities provide opportunities to meet prospective clients and begin forming relationships with them. The networking phase identifies prospects and sets up the third phase, the one-on-meetings in the final layer, the target phase.

Target phase. The funnel is the narrowest at this final phase, emblematic of the focus here – strengthening relationships with bona fide sales targets and moving those relationships to one-on-one meetings at which specific messages are delivered to decision-makers, and the CPA asks for the order.

Marketing Funnel

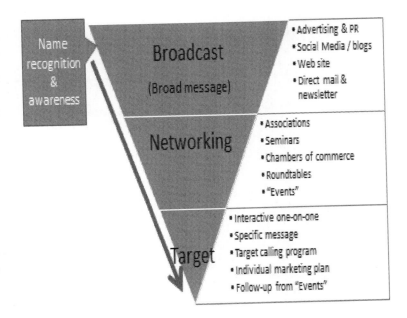

Where CPA firms get their clients

The percentages vary from firm to firm, but throughout my 20+ years of working with CPA firms, I have found the following to be reliable:

	Percentage of New Business for Firms
Existing clients that make referrals to other companies and request expanded services.	60%
Referral sources (lawyers, bankers)	30%
New clients from the firm's marketing and practice development efforts.	10%

The similarities between McDonalds and CPA firms

The following chart illustrates the three main sales strategies for McDonald's restaurants. Pretty close to CPA firms:

	McDonald's	CPA
1	Get more customers to come into the restaurant.	Get more clients; new clients.
2	"Would you like fries and an apple pie with your Big Mac?"	Cross-selling: • The firm is hired for an audit and later, gets the opportunity to do tax work. • The firm is hired for accounting work and later, is asked to assist the client acquire a business.
3	The same customers visit the restaurant more often.	Because of providing great service and making available a wide diversity of services, the CPA is retained year after year.

The CPA firm marketing plan: The Four Disciplines

This methodology is courtesy of our friends at The Growth Partnership, a St. Louis-based CPA consulting firm that specializes in marketing, leadership development and practice management.

GETTING STARTED: THE FIRST STEPS

- Create the firm's vision
- Differentiate your firm from the competition
- Best differentiator: Specialties and niches
- A credible partner must become the marketing champion of the firm

DISCIPLINE 1: MINING EXISTING CLIENTS	DISCIPLINE 2: STIMULATING REFERRAL SOURCES
<ul><li>Identify clients to meet with</li><li>Prepare a report summarizing issues the client needs to address</li><li>Client satisfaction survey</li><li>Lost client interviews</li></ul>	<ul><li>Identify firms to meet with</li><li>Track inbound and outbound referrals</li><li>Periodic "events" with referral sources that have potential.</li></ul>
DISCIPLINE 3: ATTRACTING NEW CLIENTS	**DISCIPLINE 4: PROMOTING THE FIRM**
<ul><li>Direct mail campaigns</li><li>Networking in organizations, associations, etc. with follow-up</li><li>Roundtable groups</li><li>Seminars and speaking</li><li>Writing articles & blogging</li></ul>	<ul><li>Web site and brochures</li><li>Advertising and press releases</li><li>Industry surveys</li><li>Client testimonials</li><li>Industry specialties and niches</li></ul>

SYSTEMS THAT ENABLE ACTIONS FROM THE 4 DISCIPLINES

- Training in practice development
- Mentoring/coaching
- Marketing budget established
- Internal marketing director

- Accountability established
- Incentives for practice development
- External marketing consultants
- Marketing plans for individuals

18 ways that CPAs make rain

It's common for CPAs to be uncomfortable with practice development. But as we've stated throughout this chapter, it's critical to the success of the firm. Everyone doesn't need to be a rainmaker. Here are 18 ways that shy, introverted people can help their firms grow:

1. **ATTITUDE.** All of the techniques that follow may not be possible if you don't approach practice development with the right attitude. You've got to have a conversation with yourself and pound into your head how important it is to bring in business and how your career in public accounting will be so much more successful once you develop practice development skills.

    -   It's the quickest path to becoming successful in public accounting.

    -   It's the most effective way to make great money in public accounting.

    -   Regardless of how strong you are technically, your skills will serve little purpose unless you have clients to provide services *to*.

    -   Your approach to practice development should be this: you are looking for opportunities to create win-win relationships with prospective clients. A win-win relationship is one in which both your firm and the client receive substantial benefits: the firm gets the business and the client receives services that improve their company and make their lives better. You shouldn't seek relationships that are one-sided – you get your firm hired and the client derives little benefit.

2. **Watch the "stars" play**. In sports, highly touted rookies are often asked to sit on the bench for a while to learn how the game is played by watching the stars. The same applies to practice development. Watch how the rainmaking partners in your firm do it. Observe their style. Bug them repeatedly to take you out with them on sales pitches. Pester them to reveal their "Houdini-type" tricks.

3. **Training. Training. Training.** Some feel that a person is either born a marketer or not, and that those who are not can never be trained to be effective business getters. These people are dead wrong! Most people can always get better at practice development by attending marketing conferences, reading books and articles about sales and attending sales training programs. When it comes to acquiring very difficult skills like selling, most of us need to hear the same things over and over and over again. At some point, it sinks in.

4. **Pledging**. This is a term introduced to me by a managing partner many years ago. He said that at some point, after watching the stars and getting your training, you've got to muster up the courage to start practicing your selling. He called this pledging. As Nike says: "Just do it." In perfecting practice development skills, there is no substitute for practicing it in front of real customers as often as you can. You can't be afraid of making mistakes or feeling foolish, because most everyone has similar experiences before hitting their stride. After a while, you will begin to develop your own personal style. Then, one day, after you've completed a pitch, it will dawn on you that you're done pledging. You know how to do it now! But it all starts with pledging.

5. **Become "famous."** Once you've made a name for yourself prospective clients seek *you* out and you can pull back on your proactive selling. What do we mean by "famous?" You don't have to become a reality show star. Instead, you engage in various activities on a continuous basis over many years that gets your name in front of people you want as clients.

61

6. **Specialization.** The best and easiest way to make rain is to develop a specialty in a service and/or industry. By making speeches in your area of expertise, writing articles, blogging, conducting surveys, etc., you will eventually become well-known in the specialty field. The best way to <u>beat</u> the competition is to have <u>no</u> competition. If you are perceived as one of the top providers in your niche, you no longer compete on price. All good things!

7. **Networking.** The more people you meet, the more you increase your chances of getting a client or a referral source. Common forms of networking include joining organizations, attending charity events, school reunions, churches and synagogues, roundtable groups, getting to know fellow parents on your child's athletic teams and staying in touch with old school chums

8. **"If you don't ask, you don't get."** This is where the rubber meets the road for most CPAs. Once you've developed the right attitude and actually managed to form a relationship with a prospective client, there still is one more major step that is needed: <u>Ask for the order</u>. Don't assume that simply because you succeeded at forming a nice relationship with a prospect and that you can legitimately satisfy the prospect's need, that the company will automatically hire you. You've got to push it to the next level and ask for the order.

9. **The ideal day**. Let me start with what the *wrong* day is. The wrong day is getting dressed in the morning and looking forward to arriving at the office early and getting started on the nine hours of billable work you have for the day. You order in lunch so you don't have to leave your desk. Then, just before you leave the office at night, the highlight of the day arrives: You get to type in the number "9" in your timesheet for the day's billable hours.

What's missing from this picture? There is no contact with people. Not with staff. Not with clients. Not with prospects and referral sources.

The ideal day is a blend of "people activities" and doing your work. The ideal day recognizes that you can't wait until 12 noon to find a client or prospect to invite to lunch. The ideal day recognizes that the morning hour of 9am to 10 am is the best time to reach someone to schedule a future appointment.

10. **Make money by getting rejected.** Sounds counterintuitive, doesn't it? Learn that when clients or prospects say "no" to your selling efforts, they may really be saying "not yet." Learn that on average you'll hear four "no's" for every "yes" you get. So, when someone says "no," keep in mind that your odds of getting a "yes" on the next attempt just increased! You must be persistent to make the odds work in your favor.

11. **Learn the fine art of elevator talk.** Andy Warhol famously said that everyone will have their 15 minutes of fame. Sometimes 15 seconds may be all you get when presented with an unexpected sales opportunity...like meeting someone in the elevator of your office building. So, have a rehearsed-yet-spontaneous-sounding spiel ready when you're meeting someone. Make sure that your spiel focuses on...

12. **How your firm is different from other CPA firms.** It could be a strong specialty. An audit focus. State of the art use of computers. Incredibly efficient processes. There must be *something* about your firm that is special. Avoid at all costs telling someone what you do in a way that makes you sound like every other CPA in town.

13. **Maximize your times at bat.** Practice development is a contact sport. The more sales opportunities you get, the more clients will result. If you have one sales opportunity a quarter, and you land two new clients a year from it, in baseball parlance, that's a .500 batting average – pretty darned good. But you have only two new clients. However, if you get one sales opportunity *per month*, and close a third of them, though your batting average falls to .333, you have four new clients, instead of just two. The more at-bats, the more hits you will get.

14. **Cultivate your present clients.** Roughly 60% of all new business at CPA firms comes from their existing clients in the form of expanded services or referrals to others. Sure, it's great to get new clients, but it's much easier to get more business from satisfied existing clients.

15. **Get your clients to say "Oh, wow."** One of the best sources of referrals is from your existing clients. But they will only make those referrals if you give them a reason to do so – providing great quality service and satisfying all their needs. So, figure out ways to create the "Oh Wow" response from your clients when you work with them.

16. **Learn to listen.** Resist the temptation to do a lot of talking when you are with a prospective client or referral source. Aim to do no more than 20% of the talking so that the prospect does 80%. Remember, the letters in the word "listen" can be rearranged to spell "silent."

17. **WIIFM.** When you are doing your 20% talking, remember that every second you talk, the prospect is asking him/herself: "What's in it for me," which, if you take the first letter of each of those words, spells WIIFM.

18. **Have fun.** I close with "have fun" because it came from one of the best rainmaking managing/founding partners I have ever known. He told me that as people do the types of things listed in this chart, they should always remember one thing: "Marketing is fun!" Make sure that whatever you do to bring in business, that you have fun doing it. It's contagious.

Mining the gold in your backyard: Your *existing* client base

Prospecting for new clients is an important practice development activity for all CPA firms. It's much easier to increase revenue from your *existing* clients than seeking business from people you don't know. Your clients know you and you know them. The vast majority of them would be happy to meet with you to discuss the following:

- Can you introduce us to any other companies or individuals?

- Does your company need any additional services that our firm provides?

There is one critically important step that must be done before you can ask the above: You must create the "Oh Wow" response from your clients on the work you do for them. If you haven't done this, then it's unlikely that your clients will help you out.

Here are some techniques for creating the "Oh Wow" response:

- Frequent contact, even when you're not working on an ongoing project for them.
- *Exceed* your clients' expectations. Example: Complete a client project ahead of schedule.
- Every now and then, give away some time.
- *Initiate* phone calls to clients instead of waiting for *them* to call.
- No fee surprises.
- Learn your clients' industries.
- Make unsolicited referrals to your clients.
- Keep clients informed of outside events and developments that affect them.
- Entertain them.
- Show interest in the client beyond the business relationship.
- Recognize the clients' honors, awards, etc.
- Ask your clients periodically how you can do a better job.

7

How CPA Firms
Are Managed

Two kinds of firms

Some might argue that not much really *needs* to be managed at a CPA firm. These cynics might say: "Come on. Running a CPA firm isn't rocket science. You hang out your shingle. You get clients. You do the work. Bill and collect. And that's just about it."

Unfortunately, many CPA firm partners think this way. They may not do it consciously, but it happens nonetheless. When firms learn that the lack of commitment to firm management as typified by the above attitude creates problems, they often hire consultants like me to help them address these issues:

- High staff turnover.
- Partners work like Lone Rangers; no teamwork.
- Partners complain that the firm never has enough staff and definitely doesn't have *the right* staff.
- Unreliable computer systems.
- Bills go out late and are collected even later.
- The firm's policies and procedures vary according to which partner you ask.
- Revenues and profits stagnate and disappoint.

The other school of thought acknowledges that CPA firms are just like other businesses: To be successful, these areas must be managed effectively:

- **Human resource issues:** Staff must be recruited, trained and supervised effectively in order to provide partners with competent support.

- **Marketing and practice development:** Clients aren't hanging on trees like low-lying fruit, waiting to be picked. Bringing in clients is extremely difficult for most CPAs. To be successful at it, the firm needs a marketing plan and accountability for practice development.

- **Systems and technology:** Computers have revolutionized how client work is done. These days, if the firm's power goes out, people have to go home – that's how much they rely on their computers. Providing the firm with access to current technology and the systems that go along with it requires a substantial commitment by firm management.

- **Administrative duties:** If partners must routinely tend to the myriad of administrative tasks required to run a firm, their available time to bring in business, do client work and mentor the staff is greatly reduced. Firms need competent, experienced people like firm administrators, marketing directors, HR specialists and IT directors to keep the firm operating on a day to day basis.

- **Managing partner:** And finally, to insure that all of the above are done expertly, and at the same time, prevent the partners from killing each other, the firm needs *someone* to serve as the leader. Managing partners usually fill this bill.

Overarching philosophies for managing a CPA firm

Accounting firms generally gravitate to one or the other extreme for each of the following areas:

1. **Partnership vs. corporate style.**
   - The partnership style is very much a democratic style. All partners are involved in all decisions, large and small. They vote on everything. They split up the admin duties so everyone does their share. No partner would ever be trusted to make decisions for all partners.

   - Corporate style. A CPA firm is a business and needs to be managed like one. Partners do two things: take care of clients and take care of staff. Leave the firm's management to professionals hired for this purpose. Very few votes are ever taken because authority for making most day to day decisions is vested with management, not the partners.

2. **Operating as a team vs. a bunch of Lone Rangers.** Teamwork is the belief that the firm can achieve more when people work together as a team. Lone Rangers generally work alone and achieve success mostly as a result of their own individual efforts.

3. **Adherence to a set of core values.** Attitudes and beliefs define the firm's culture. Core values are what the firm stands for, what is held dear and what the partners believe in. The acid test of whether or not a firm truly has a set of core values is the extent to which transgressions are allowed. If partners are free to define their own core values, and allowed to violate these values willy-nilly, then there really are <u>no</u> core values.

4. **Is the firm driven by production or a strategic vision?** Most firms agree that strategic planning is important. Some never allow the pursuit of the strategic plan to be trumped by production (bringing in business and working billable hours). Others value production above all else, feeling that strategic planning is to be done when one has spare time.

What needs to be managed?

Strategic planning	The firm is driven by a vision of what the partners would like the firm to look like in 5 or 10 years.
Productivity	<ul><li>Keeping staff busy; formal scheduling of staff.</li><li>Achieving individual targets for charge hours.</li><li>Achieving standards for quality of work.</li><li>Effective use of non-billable time.</li></ul>
Processes	Will the firm do its work the same way, regardless of who is in charge of the client project? Or will the firm allow each partner to "do it their way?" Examples: Doing an audit Doing a tax return Filing for an extension Doing an inventory physical Client billing Filling out a timesheet
Administration	Renting office space Billing system & collections Internal accounting Insurance Paying bills Budgeting Office equipment Firm policies
Quality control	Creation of written policies and standards for doing audit, accounting and tax work. Also includes procedures to test firm personnel's compliance with the firm's standards.
Human resources/staff issues	Compensation Benefits Personnel policies Training Orientation Mentoring Feedback Promotions Recruiting/hiring
Marketing of the firm	Marketing is all the things a firm does to promote the firm and get name recognition. Examples: branding, brochures, direct mail, seminars, give speeches, write articles, etc.
Technology	<ul><li>A dozen or so CPA firm-specific software programs</li><li>Security, privacy, client portals</li><li>Mobile devices, remote access</li></ul>

ORGANIZATION CHARTS

SMALL FIRM
2-5 PARTNERS/6-20 PEOPLE

MEDIUM-SIZED FIRM
6-10 PARTNERS/20-50 PEOPLE

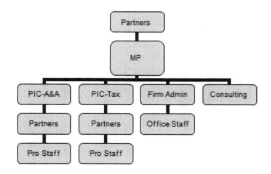

LARGE FIRM
OVER 10 PARTNERS & OVER 50 PEOPLE

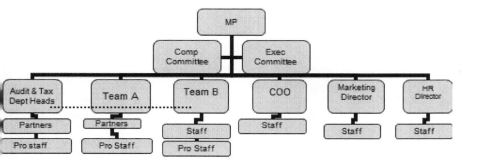

71

25 BEST PRACTICES OF THE MOST SUCCESSFUL FIRMS

These 25 best practices have been extracted from Rosenberg's work with great firms over the past 20 years. Few firms do them all, but the best firms do most of them.

1.	The firm's culture is the #1 success factor. Author Jim Collins coined this by saying: Get the right people ON the bus and the wrong people OFF the bus.
2.	Proactive business-getting efforts.
3.	Exploit potential with existing clients.
4.	Develop specialized expertise and niches.
5.	World class service.
6.	Be high price-low-volume rather than low price-high volume.
7.	Effective management structure & leadership.
8.	Franchised procedures. Everyone performs the firm's major work processes *the same way.*
9.	Clients are institutionalized, served by teams, not Lone Rangers.
10.	Partners focus on clients and staff, staying out of administration.
11.	Survey clients and staff to find out what they think of you.
12.	Maximize staff to partner leverage; partners are delegators.
13.	Clear strategic plan. Vision. Direction. Implementation.
14.	Diversity of services.
15.	Tenacious commitment to make the firm a great place to work.
16.	Partners are good bosses and effective at mentoring the staff.
17.	Proactive leadership development.
18.	World class training.
19.	Succession planning.
20.	Personnel conflicts are quickly addressed and resolved.
21.	All personnel accountable for their performance and behavior.
22.	All partners and staff should have targets and goals.
23.	All partners and staff are compensated based on performance.
24.	Put technology to work for you, including use of social media.
25.	Constantly benchmark the firm against industry norms.

8

How Staff Can Have a Great Career in Public Accounting

What recruits should learn from their CPA firm interviews

Interviewing at CPA firms can be a daunting, anxious time for job candidates. For many, this may be the first time in their adult life when they will be judged and evaluated based on their personality and communication skills, not just strictly on grades.

Not all CPA firms are alike. When interviewing with a CPA firm, don't assume anything. Don't accept firms' descriptions of themselves as 100% factual; firms, just like job candidates, tend to oversell themselves.

Use your interview with a firm to fully understand its culture and how it operates. Learn the following about firms you interview with:

1. The firm's training of staff:
   - Is the majority of training live vs. media or self-study?
   - In addition to technical accounting and tax is there a meaningful amount of soft skills and software training as well?
   - Has the firm developed a customized training program as opposed to "one size fits all" training?
   - Does the firm have a mentoring program? Ask the firm to describe it.

- Find out about new employee orientation:
  - When does it begin? (should be <u>before</u> your first day).
  - What does it consist of?
  - How long does it last? (bad answer is that it consists of someone taking you out to lunch on your first day).

2. Technology:
   - The firm's technology should be current.
   - It should be clear that partners are good with computers and use them often. Bad sign: "older" partners who hardly know how to turn their computers on.
   - Paperless technology should be rampant.

3. Ages of the partners:
   - Ideally there should be a nice spread from older to younger. The more partners in their 30s and 40s, the better.
   - Ask when the last time someone was promoted to partner from entry level staff; beware if this hardly ever happens.
   - When was the last time *anyone* was made partner; if it wasn't in the last several years, this could be a signal of stagnation.
   - Ask them what their succession plan is:
     - Older partners turn the firm over to younger partners and retire at a traditional retirement age, or...
     - Eventually merge with a bigger firm, or...
     - Partners never want to retire and work well into their late 60s and 70s (means there is little room for new partners).

4. The firm's staff:
   - What is the firm's ratio of professional staff to partner – the higher the better, but anything less than 3 to 1 means the partners do too much work that the staff should do.
   - What is the staff turnover? (Above 20% not good)
   - How long does it take before entry level staff has meaningful contact with clients? (right answer is right away)
   - What is the dress code? The vast majority of firms are 100% casual. Anything different indicates stodginess.
   - What are my advancement and promotion opportunities?

5. Questions about the firm:
   - What has been the firm's growth rate been the last 2-3 years?
   - What does the firm do to promote itself?

What it takes to be a successful staff person in a CPA firm

In the previous section, we said that interviewing for a job at a CPA firm may be the first time in your adult life that you are evaluated based on your personality, not just your grades.

This continues once you are hired and start working at the firm. Sure, performing your work with accuracy and thoroughness is important, and you need to work hard to achieve this performance attribute. But in determining your overall success at the firm, the following will be considered at least as important as the technical quality of your work:

1. Interpersonal and communication skills, both with clients and firm personnel:

   - Write articulate, coherent emails.
   - Gain the confidence of the client. Try to work as much as possible in the field - that's where you learn.
   - Learn the client's business, not just their accounting systems.
   - Litmus test of when clients are comfortable and confident of you: clients call you instead of your supervisor.

2. Be a self-starter; develop a reputation for reliability; someone who gets things done:

   - Take responsibility for the job from beginning to end.
   - Leadership: take ownership of the project or situation.
   - Before going to the supervisor for help, try to solve the problem yourself – but don't spin your wheels.
   - Be able to apply your knowledge in unusual projects/situations and solve the problem.
   - NEVER, EVER submit work for review, knowing it needs further work, expecting the supervisor to correct it or finish it.

3. Demonstrate that you are passionate about your job and your work. If you see a confusing or perplexing issue, pounce on it; don't ignore it and don't dump it in the supervisor's laps.

4. Ask lots of questions, but show that you've given thought to it first.

5. Don't spin your wheels. Avoid amassing hours and hours of work on a project when you don't really understand what you're doing, only to find out that the work is incorrect and has to be re-done.

6. Always know what the time budgets and deadlines are for your assignments. Ask if you're not told. Right away.

7. Ask what the firm expects of you in terms of annual billable hours and realization.

8. Be proactive in finding work with supervisors when you have unassigned blocks in your calendar. If on Friday, you know you have no work for the following Wednesday, don't wait until Wednesday morning to ask around for work.

9. Ask for performance feedback after every job; don't wait until the supervisor gets around to it. Don't try to "escape" without getting the feedback or asking for feedback, figuring (incorrectly) that what you don't know won't hurt you.

10. It's OK to strive for work-life balance, but understand that meeting clients' needs comes first.

11. Proficiency with technology.

12. Learn all the services your firm provides so you can spot additional opportunities for the firm to help the client.

13. Self-confidence. Don't hide from partners. Gain *their* confidence. Partners like to see young staff be assertive and comfortable making conversation with older adults. Turn them into mentors.

14. Show ambition. Always know what it takes to get ahead, but make sure you master present duties before you ask for advancement.

15. Think "the firm," not "me."

16. Oh yes... Master the technical requirements of your job. (This is really a "given.").

The primary staff positions in a CPA firm and what it takes to advance

There is no standard set of titles or positions at CPA firms. But these four designations are very common at most firms:

STAFF

Core of the position:	To advance:
• Entry level	• Ability to "run" small jobs
• Learning technical skills; lots of review notes; close supervision	• Command of basic technical work; doesn't repeat mistakes; reliable.
• Almost always reports to a level below partner	• Hits annual charge hour budget with acceptable realization
• One job at a time	• Works well with clients & co-workers.
• Does not supervise staff	• Generally, 2-3 years as a staff person

SENIOR

Core of the position:	To advance:
• Handles almost all technical issues; minimal review notes	• Delivers jobs to manager or partner with minimal changes required
• Delivers job to next level complete; runs jobs in the field	• Skillful supervisor
	• Credibility with staff and partners
• Reports to a partner on some jobs	• Productive and realizable
• One job at a time	• Demonstrates potential to be a partner or a manager.
• Supervises staff	
• Decent amount of client contact	• 2-3 years as a senior
• Begins to get active in practice development activities	

MANAGER

Core of the position:	To advance:
• 1st line duties in engagement management, including billing, collection and project budgeting.	• Excels at handling complex jobs
	• Practice development success
• Approaches partners in terms of technical skill level.	• High level of trust and credibility with both staff and partners
• Delivers jobs to partner so thorough that partner review is only high spot	• Able to manage a client base
	• Can control client relationships
• Several jobs at once	• Willing/able to buy-in as a partner
• Supervises staff and mentors them	• Firm has enough revenues to justify adding a partner
• Meaningful client relationships	
• Ratcheting up of PD activity	• 3-5 years as a manager

PARTNER

• <u>Drives</u> growth & profits	• Brings in business, year after year
• A strong leader; sets a good example, in & outside of the firm	• Active in PD *activities*
• Manages client relationships	• May have internal management duties/positions
• High client retention rate	• Keeps staff busy; pushes billable hours to lowest level; leverages his/her time
• Cross-sells	
• Cultivates referral sources	• Oversees technical aspect of jobs
• Command a partner level billing rate	• Often a specialist in *something*
• Staff advance under his/her tutelage	• Lives & breathes the firm's core values every day

General performance traits needed to advance (regardless of the position you aspire to)

BASICS	WILD CARDS*
1. Learn well, absorb what you are taught; get your work done accurately and presentably.	1. Bring in clients. 2. Develop a specialty.
2. Complete your work within the number of hours expected.	
3. Complete your work on time.	* "Wild cards" are clearly skills that all CPA firms would love their staff to develop. However, as a practical matter, many staff have difficulty developing them. Indeed, many *partners* don't develop them.
4. Complete your work so thoroughly that it seldom needs to be changed.	
5. Proficiency with technology.	Some firms require these skills to be considered for partner while many others say "it would be great if our staff could acquire these skills but we will stop short of requiring them to make partner."
6. Stay busy with client work.	
7. Develop effective interpersonal and communication skills.	
8. Supervise staff effectively; train them and help them grow.	
9. Work on multiple jobs at the same time.	
10. Develop effective relationships with clients.	
11. Technical excellence.	
12. Show passion and enthusiasm for your work.	

Quality of supervision that staff should expect from their firm

These are the traits you should experience from good supervisors	These are unacceptable supervisory practices
1. Made me feel like an equal and respects me.	1. Disrespectful; talked down to me.
2. Timely and constructive feedback.	2. "No news is good news" approach to giving feedback.
3. Supervisor feedback addresses your performance without making it personal.	3. Criticizes your work in public.
4. Open and accessible for questions.	4. Poor planning; things always done last minute.
5. Gave me some rope; didn't micromanage me.	5. Unrealistic expectations. Expected me to do work way over my head without any training.
6. Gave me good instructions.	6. Unfairly rigid; a "my way or the highway" type of person.
7. Receptive to my ideas and suggestions.	7. Lack of honesty.
8. Gives me the chance to make changes based on review of my work.	8. Takes credit for my accomplishments and blames me for things beyond my control.
	9. Doesn't respect my time; takes phone calls when I'm in his office.

World class client service to which ALL staff should aspire

1. Summarize all client meetings in writing and list action items resulting from meeting. Establish specific agenda and goals prior to meeting. Send it out within 2-3 days of the meeting.

2. Follow-up with the client regarding progress on commitments.

3. Be proactive. Even if client didn't hire you for business advice, give opinions on how to improve their company as you observe them.

4. Periodically visit with client outside confines of routine engagement in an effort to understand client's problems and give suggestions.

5. Make reports more valuable. Use graphics.

6. Access: Give clients your home phone numbers, e-mail addresses, etc.

7. Complete work *before* it is due.

8. Always return phone calls and emails promptly.

9. Ensure that client knows whom to call if you aren't accessible.

10. If client asks a question you can't answer, take immediate initiative to resolve the question promptly by getting others involved.

11. No surprises – with either the client report or the bill.

12. Make referrals *to* your client. Make introductions.

13. Email links to your clients of interesting articles and information. Alternatively, clip and mail them.

14. Perform as much work as possible in the clients' office.

9

How CPA Firms Attract and Retain Staff

The AICPA recently conducted a survey of what attracts staff to CPA firms and what enables firms to retain them. The survey was conducted for staff as well as partners so that the responses of the two groups could be compared to each other.

The survey results are summarized in the chart at the end of this chapter.

The main observations are:

1. Never underestimate the importance of compensation. No one thinks it is unimportant, but a lot of people seem to think it's not as high on the list of what staff most wants. This survey confirms what numerous surveys have shown in recent years – salary rates very high with staff.

2. Career growth opportunities run neck and neck with salary. It is critical that firms demonstrate to recruits as well as existing staff that there is a career path for them in your firm. It's equally important that you mentor staff –show you intend to help them along the way instead of sitting back and waiting for them to show they have "the right stuff."

But it's not enough *to talk* to the staff about career growth opportunities. The firm must demonstrate by <u>actions it takes</u> that the firm is going places and that they have a future with the firm.

Examples of these actions:

- Revenue growth and a steady stream of exciting new clients.

- Allow staff input in the firm's strategic plan, which is publicized firm-wide and followed religiously.

- Creation of a bold marketing plan that fosters an image of respect and admiration in the marketplace. It should be "cool" to work for your firm.

- Differentiation from other CPA firms through areas such as specialization, personalized training programs, staff mentoring, technological innovation, etc.

- Proactive leadership development programs for the staff; both internal and external programs.

- Written documentation of what it takes to advance from position to position. Don't make it a mystery how one advances in your firm.

3. It's surprising how low flexible work schedule shows in this survey. Many surveys of what employees want show that a flexible work schedule is very high on their list; they want to be judged on whether or not they did their job on a timely basis instead of when and where the hours were worked. Apparently, someone forgot to tell this to the staff participating in this survey.

AICPA/PCPS 2011 Top Talent Survey
What Attracts and Retains Staff
December, 2011

Rank	Attraction Factors	Staff 2011	Staff 2006	Partners 2011
	Career growth opportunities	91%	80%	84%
	Salary	88%	78%	90%
	Paid personal/vacation time	86%	79%	83%
	Open-door/accessible management	83%	68%	74%
	Comfortable office atmosphere	81%	69%	77%
	Interesting, challenging client projects	81%	71%	77%
	Medical benefits	73%	70%	71%
	Firm's reputation or prestige	73%	59%	78%
	Retirement savings plan	72%	67%	61%
	CPE credit reimbursement	65%	50%	58%
	Paid sick days	60%	55%	
	Flexible work schedule	59%	65%	
	Access to cutting-edge technology	57%	52%	
	Regular performance reviews/feedback	50%	40%	

Rank	Retention Factors	Staff 2011	Staff 2006	Partners 2011
	Salary	95%	89%	88%
	Career growth opportunities	93%	92%	83%
	Paid personal/vacation time	90%	86%	84%
	Open-door/accessible management	89%	89%	83%
	Interesting, challenging client projects	88%	88%	84%
	Comfortable office atmosphere	87%	83%	82%
	Firm's reputation or prestige	79%	74%	80%
	Flexible work schedule	78%	88%	76%
	Retirement savings plan	77%	78%	64%
	Frequent client contact	76%	74%	73%
	Team-orientation of firm	72%	75%	
	CPE credit reimbursement	67%	57%	
	Telecommuting/work from home options	63%	67%	
	Interesting, challenging internal projects	59%	88%	

10

100 Years of Game-Changing Milestones & Eye-Opening Innovations

Yes, you're reading the title of this chapter correctly. My description of major industry milestones and innovations as "game-changing" and "eye-opening" will be received with skepticism by most who read this chapter.

In researching this material I uncovered a fascinating disconnect: If you ask CPA firm partners, as I did, if they consider CPA firms to be innovative, there is very little hesitation in their response: no and no, in that order.

However, the following timeline of major innovations tells a different story. There is no question that the profession has undergone significant change in the past 100 years. The list of key industry advancements will show how truly innovative CPA firms have been in the last 20-30 years.

Brief history of major milestones in the CPA profession

- 1913   - Federal income tax created.
- 1933-34 -SEC Acts created
- 1941-45 - U.S. starts income tax withholding.
- 1978   - Bates decision – accountants now allowed to solicit.
- 1979   - Visi-Calc introduced (the first spreadsheet).
- Early '80s Firm administrator concept gains traction.
- Early '80s – PC revolution begins.
- Mid   '80s – Regional and local firms increase consulting services - formerly the sole bastion of large nationals.
- 1988 – CPAs allowed to receive commissions & contingent fees.
- 1988 – Arthur Andersen civil war (CPA vs. consulting) begins.
- 1989 – Big 8 loses 2 firms to mergers.
- 1991 – Dawning of the internet age.
- 1993 – 30 states pass 150 hour rule.
- 1993 – Email begins.
- 1994 – Non-CPA partners allowed.
- 1994 – CPA firms allowed to incorporate.
- 1995 – Barry Melancon takes over as Chief of AICPA
- 1996 – Investment advisory services launched.
- 1997/98 – Consolidator movement begins in earnest.
- 2000 – Andersen Consulting divorces from Arthur Andersen.
- 2000 – Since 1995, 33% reduction in number of college accounting majors in the U.S.
- 2000 - AICPA tries to replace "CPA" with "Cognitor." It fails.
- 2000 – 150 hour rule now universal in all states.
- 2001 – Enron bankruptcy.
- 2001 – Paperless office concept starts gaining traction.
- 2002 – Andersen collapses.
- 2002 – SOX and PCAOB – the death of self-regulation for CPAs.
- 2002 – Big 4 starts selling off their consulting practices.
- 2002 – CPA firms create "mentoring" programs.
- 2003 – Golden Era of CPA firm revenue boom begins, triggered by SOX and trickle-down. New billion dollar service launched – Section 404 work.
- 2003 – Outsourcing tax returns to India begins.
- 2004 – Uniform CPA Exam in computerized format; the end of paper and pencil.

- 2005 – SEC and European Commission set up road map to converge standards by 2009 (never happened).
- 2005 – Supreme Court overturns Andersen conviction.
- 2006 - AICPA moves most of its HQ in New York to N. Carolina.
- 2007 – SEC and PCAOB offer new guidelines to reduce cost of Section 404 audits.
- 2005 - Merger mania. Some large regionals becoming national.
- 2008-2010 – Worst recession since the Great Depression. CPA firm's motto: "Flat is up."
- 2009 - "Big GAAP, Little GAAP" hotly debated and totally unresolved.
- 2009- Adoption of IFRS in the U.S. nowhere in sight.
- 2011 – IRS establishes Registered Tax Preparer designation.
- 2011 – Gallup poll on honesty and ethics among professionals shows accountants regaining their lofty status prior to the Enron/Andersen debacles.
- 2012-2013- Fiscal cliff drama leading to a brutal 2013 tax season.
- 2013 – IRS tax preparer regulation ruled unconstitutional.

CPA firms lacking innovation? Think again

Leaders in our profession see CPA firms as being reactive rather than proactive. Indeed, most managing partners and reputable consultants to the profession feel there have been few industry innovations outside of technology.

Yet an impressive array of innovations has occurred in the past 20 years. One can't help but conclude that the CPA profession has embraced change as much as any other profession.

Here's what Barry Melancon, President and CEO of the AICPA had to say on this topic:

"Innovation has been much more prevalent than some will say. I truly believe the CPA profession gets a bad rap on innovation. Don't let anyone tell you that CPAs don't innovate. I'd argue not only that they do it, but they do it in a reasoned and thoughtful way."

15 impressive CPA firm innovations

The items below are listed in order of significance to the public accounting profession, in the author's opinion.

1. **Technology.** Clearly, this is THE primary area of innovation for CPA firms in the past 20 years, paralleling the evolution of the PC. The way accountants do their work has been <u>totally</u> transformed and continues to change rapidly, <u>every year</u>. CPAs have been quick to embrace technology. Here are the major innovations according to the CPA profession's leading technology expert, Roman Kepczyk of Xcentric:

   a. Internet.
   b. Email.
   c. Windows graphical interface, which along with word processing software, eliminated the typing pool.
   d. Microsoft Office.
   e. Multiple screen/monitor displays – made possible a huge jump in individual productivity.
   f. Smartphones and tablets, including the touch screen.
   g. The "Cloud," including portals and addressing of security issues.
   h. Workflow, including paperless audit and scanning technology.
   i. Social networking –more an emerging technology because it has yet to have a big impact for CPA firms.

2. **Shift in focus from the client to firms' people.** Years ago, firms were almost totally client focused, viewing people somewhat as a commodity. That has changed drastically because of the terrible shortage of talented labor and the massive retirement of Baby Boomer partners. People at firms are now the single most important factor in their success.

3. **Pro-active marketing of CPA firm services.** Although the Bates case in the late 1970s freed accountants to solicit, CPAs selling services didn't begin in earnest until years later. In recent years, CPA firms have caught on to branding as a marketing tactic and a few firms have hired sales professionals to sell and make calls. Marketing of CPA firm services has transformed the way firms are managed.

4. **Business consulting.** Tagline of the old days: ABC Firm-CPAs. Today: ABC Firm – CPAs *and Consultants.*

   CPAs don't *just* do accounting and tax; they do consulting as well. These three main services are delivered to clients almost seamlessly, all in the name of satisfying as many of their clients' needs as possible. A whole new buzz word was created for this: one-stop shopping – the CPA firm as the <u>one place</u> where clients and referral sources can have all their needs met.

5. **Specialization and niche marketing.** CPAs were behind the doctors and lawyers on this one, but they are now catching on.

6. **Mentoring** and **Leadership Development.** The buzz words emblematic of the paradigm shift in CPA firms' mindset: instead of waiting for staff to develop the "right stuff" <u>on their own</u>, as the Baby Boomers were expected to, firms are now proactive in helping staff learn and grow.

7. **Wealth management.** In the 1990s, CPA firms woke up and realized that they were their clients' most trusted advisors - more than lawyers, bankers and others. Firms tapped into this by providing wealth management services.

8. **Training:**
   a. **Curriculum-based, university-type training** by firms, replacing the traditional, somewhat haphazard cornucopia of ineffective, outside seminars and canned videos that used to be firms' training mainstay.

   b. **Soft-skills training** is now an integral part of firms' overall training whereas 10-15 years or more ago, 99+% of all training was technical A&A and tax.

9. **Internships** are now the primary way firms hire entry-level staff.

10. **Abandonment of the "up or out"** policy for staff. The profession had no choice as interest in accounting as a college major has shrunk dramatically since the mid-1990s.

11. **Flex-time and part-time partner policies.** As the ranks of available staff shrunk dramatically, and the percentage of female accounting majors swelled beyond 50%, firms have learned to accommodate the needs of women.

12. **Partner compensation systems moving from 100% production to systems requiring partners to be more well-rounded.** Archaic production formulas are increasingly being replaced by partner compensation systems that recognize the importance of intangible attributes like firm management, helping staff learn and grow and teamwork.

13. **COOs and directors of marketing, HR and IT** handle the bulk of the firm's day to day management instead of the partners.

14. **Self-imposed peer review**, unmatched by any other profession.

15. CPA firms are the most **international** of all professions, according to Barry Melancon, President and CEO of the AICPA.

11

Trends in the CPA Profession

What's going on in the CPA firm industry - 2013

1. Painstakingly long duration of economic sluggishness:
   - Growth continues below 5% a year.
   - Stiff price competition among larger firms
   - Low growth rate considered to be "the new normal."

2. Firms are working hard to overcome sluggish growth:
   - Upgrading staff
   - More face-to-face with good clients
   - More marketing
   - Refocus on core values and partner accountability
   - Mergers

3. Huge overarching issues:
   - Shortage of staff
   - Retirement of Baby Boomer partners, leading to…
   - Crisis in succession planning, causing…
   - Tons of mergers

4. Succession planning:
   - Baby Boomers retiring: slim pickings for new partners
   - 61% of all partners now 50 or older
   - Long time managing partners are retiring; their firms are skipping a generation to name the next managing partner.

5. Merger sizzle:
   - Swing from sellers' to buyers' market
   - Everyone's talking to *someone*
   - Regional firms going national
   - Some saying "we're too small to be big and too big to be small."
   - Consolidation of top 100 firms

6. Growth and marketing:
   - Steady increase in larger firms bringing on sales specialists
   - Slow growth causing more firms to consider geographic expansion to increase revenues.
   - More branding
   - Larger firms: totally focused on building a deep bench, developing specialties and niches as the smart way to go to market, mentoring staff and seeking mergers.

7. Staff:
   - Accounting major in college still not "popular"
   - World-wide professor shortage prevents many universities from meeting demand for accounting classes.
   - The CPA profession has returned to its pre-recession staff shortage condition.
   - Big 4 hiring is way up
   - Salary increases rising after smaller raises during recession.
   - Major long-term trends at successful firms:
     - University or curriculum-based training, including soft skills
     - On-boarding (new employee orientation)
     - Commitment to winning "best place to work" awards
     - Staff getting two performance appraisals a year instead of just one.

8. Leadership development:

In the old days, the partners waited for the staff to show they had "the right stuff" before talking to them about becoming partners. Today, the partners are proactive in mentoring the staff and helping them become partners.

- Specifics: Formal leadership programs. Outside/inside.
- Mentoring programs.

9. Social media:
- Best for recruiting and to lesser extent, marketing
- Business case for use of social media still not clear.
- New generation defines "practice development" as getting 500 contacts on LinkedIn.

AICPA's Top 5 Issues in Managing Their Firms

This poll was conducted towards the end of 2011 and was the most recent such poll as this monograph went to print.

The numbers in each column are the relative __ranking__ of the issues.

Issue	Number of Professionals			
	Over 20	11 to 20	6 to 10	2 to 5
Partner accountability	1	2		
Bringing in new clients	2	1	1	1
Retaining clients	3	3	2	2
Fee pressure	4		5	
Succession planning	5	4		
Finding qualified staff		5		
Retaining qualified staff			3	
Tax complexity and changes			4	3
Seasonality/workload compression				4
Keeping up with prof. standards				5

A few observations:

1. Partner accountability is high on the list. Yet, it's the only one of the top five issues that is totally within firms' control and NOT impacted by external forces.

2. The emphasis on bringing in new clients is a direct result of a sluggish economy.

3. If this survey is repeated in 2013 or beyond, finding staff will probably rank #1 or #2.

4. Seasonality and workload compression hurts smaller firms more than larger ones because smaller firms focus more heavily on 1040s.

12

Ethical Issues

"Ethical guidelines are viewed in the same way as legal or accounting rules: they are constraints to be, whenever possible, circumvented or just plain ignored in the pursuit of self-interest, or in pursuit of the misconceived interest of the organization."

J. Dobson

The reality is leadership, like ethics, does exist in theory, but is only truly alive when practiced face-to-face.

Anonymous

Character: What we say and what we do when no one else is around!

Anonymous

"Our economic system rests on trust. When trust is broken, the system is damaged. Ethical behavior, then, is an intrinsic part of the bottom line."

Wm. J. Bennett

Why ethics are important

The following is excerpted from an article written by Amana Javeed for ACCA, The Global Body for Professional Accountants.

Ethics are important for Professional Accountants because throughout history, it has been proven that accounting partially reflects moral orders of the world in which it is practiced. It has become a moral discourse because of the injustice that has occurred regarding ethics in the accounting profession.

Ethics are important for Professional Accountants because accounting requires ethical knowledge and skills to a great extent. They differentiate between right and wrong. Ethics help us build personal fortitude to make the right decision. By keeping in mind ethical factors, accountants will never succumb to short term pressures for keeping up revenue growth or for satisfying investors.

Ethical behavior forces accountants to confront fraud.

Examples of unethical behavior in accounting:

1. Providing erroneous information regarding expenses incurred.
2. Exaggerating business revenue.
3. Misuse of business funds.

Examples of ethical issues commonly encountered

1. No one working at a CPA firm should EVER take shortcuts to maximize profitability or stay within the time budget if it means your work or final product will be inaccurate or in violation of professional standards and ethics.

   Example: The client is quoted a fixed fee of $10,000 for an audit. When the job is half complete, $12,000 worth of time has already been worked on the job and it looks like it will take $20,000 of time to complete a job that was quoted for $10,000. No firm personnel should EVER fail to complete the remaining audit procedures necessary to professionally and ethically issue the client audit report.

2. No supervisor in a CPA firm should assign work to a staff person who clearly lacks the experience and training to do the job properly. The one significant exception is the situation in which the supervisor uses the engagement as a teaching opportunity for the staff person. This method must include giving initial instructions and direction to the staff person, monitoring the performance of the work and completing a thorough review of the work when it is completed.

> Example: A client project last year was billed for $20,000 and $30,000 of time was incurred. One way to make the job more profitable this year is to assign the work to lower level staff with lower billing rates. However, at the same time, it is the responsibility of the firm to ensure that the staff assigned to the job have the training and experience necessary to perform the work properly.

3. Assume there is a situation in which a CPA firm performs an audit for $20,000 in fees and performs computer consulting work for $200,000 in fees. Despite the consulting work being more lucrative to the CPA firm than the audit, no firm personnel should ever perform the audit in a manner that fails to comply with professional and ethical standards.

What ethics lesson could CPAs learn from Abraham Lincoln?

As much as any historical figure, Abraham Lincoln shines brightly as a leader whose ethical standards were legendary.

In 2011 Al Gini, Professor of Business Ethics at Loyola University in Chicago presented a session on ethics to one of my Chicago CPA firm roundtable groups. He made generous use of his personal research on Abraham Lincoln to parallel ethical behavior by CPAs.

The following material is excerpted from his presentation.

Ethics deals with values relating to human conduct, with respect to the morality of certain actions and selflessness of the motives and ends of such actions.

Leadership provides proper guidance to the people in an organization to engage in the "right" conduct and have "good" motives.

- Get the politics right. Lincoln famously said: "If slavery is not wrong, what is?" Where would you take a stand with your clients and tell them what you MUST do and what you are NOT willing to do?

- Be careful about <u>what</u> and <u>how</u> you communicate.

Lincoln wrote his own speeches and was highly skilled at it. He took his public speaking very seriously. He frequently sought advice from his cabinet to make sure he communicated the right message in a sincere manner. He was famous for his story telling, which proved a very effective tactic for communicating with people on the sensitive, complex subjects of his presidency: slavery and secession.

  - How does written communication establish your leadership among firm personnel and staff on ethical issues?
  - How do you get your clients to READ what you write?
  - How do you educate your clients so that they understand the difference between right and wrong?

- Be practical, but be empathetic too. Every member of Lincoln's cabinet had more experience and education than he did. But he recognized the skills they brought to the cabinet, valued them tremendously and listened to them. What are examples of how you are open to the ideas of clients and firm personnel?

- Find your Grant. Don't try to do everything alone.

- Accept change, learn from your errors and accept responsibility. When did you last take the blame and accept responsibility?

As in most wars, many serious mistakes were made on both sides. Lincoln had minimal military training or experience and trusted his generals implicitly. But one after the other, his generals failed him. Many repeatedly refused to engage the Confederate troops despite Lincoln's direct orders to do so; he went through five or six lead generals in the early years of the war.

It took Lincoln three years to learn from his mistakes and get it right, appointing Grant in 1864. But never once did he blame anyone but himself, or shy away from the daunting responsibility of directing a long, horrific war which he was ill-equipped to direct.

Gallup Poll: An Impeccable Measure of Accountants' Reputation

I'm sure I don't need to acquaint readers with The Gallup Organization. Founded in 1935 by George Gallup, this company regularly conducts opinion polls which are often referenced in the mass media as a reliable and objective measure of public opinion.

I have been tracking one of their polls since the 1980s. It's a poll of honesty and ethics in various professions. They don't conduct the poll every year and they don't poll every profession every time they compile a survey. This poll has repeatedly shown that the public perceives accountants as among the most honest and ethical of professionals.

Gallup's polls on honesty and ethics in the professions are summarized on the next page.

Gallup Poll on Honesty and Ethics in the Professions

	2012	2011	2008	2002	2001	1991	1981
Doctors	70%	70%	64%	63%	66%	54%	50%
Engineers	70%		62%		60%	45%	48%
Police officers	58%	54%	56%	61%	68%	43%	44%
Clergy	52%	52%	56%	52%	64%	57%	63%
Accountants		**43%**	**38%**	**32%**	**41%**		
Psychiatrists	41%		33%	38%			
Bankers	28%	25%	23%	36%	34%	30%	39%
Journalists	24%	26%	25%	26%	29%	26%	32%
TV reporters		23%	23%		21%	29%	26%
Lawyers	19%	19%	18%	18%	18%	22%	25%
Senators	14%		11%	20%	25%	19%	20%
Business execs				17%	25%	18%	18%
Advertising	11%	11%	10%	9%	11%	12%	9%
Stockbrokers	11%	12%	12%	12%	19%	14%	21%
Car sales	8%	7%	7%	6%	8%	8%	6%
Telemarketers		8%	5%	5%			

Noteworthy observations:

- Accountants' honesty and ethics ratings dwarf those of almost all careers, especially those in the business world.

- Ratings for accountants plunged from 41% just prior to the Enron/Andersen fiascos of 2001 to 32% immediately afterward. Ratings have steadily increased up through 2011, when the 2001 level was surpassed.

- A favorable public perception is one of several reasons one chooses a profession. It's nice to know that your career enjoys a high degree of esteem and respect. When you tell someone you are a CPA, you get instant credibility.

13

The Image of CPAs and CPA Firms

<u>Word association game</u>

I've done this exercise dozens of times in a wide variety of settings. When one says "CPA," what words are associated with it?

We typically get three categories of responses. Here is a summary of those most commonly cited, in no particular order:

Complimentary	Viewed as positive by some and negative by others	Derogatory
• Trusted • Creative • Meticulous • Confidential • Integrity • Problem-solver • Advice • Professional • Reliable	• Rules • Details • Eccentric • Quiet • Conservative • Taxes	• Boring • Dull • Bean counter • Introvert • Nerds • Risk-aversive

CPA image problems

The complimentary side of the chart would be the envy of anyone. Coupled with great pay, an almost unlimited supply of jobs and many other attractive features, one would think that the field of public accounting would be a highly popular career choice.

But it's not:

- Although accounting as a college major is on the upswing after sinking to an historic low in 2000, it's still low by anyone's measure.

- The words on the right-hand side of the chart on the previous page clearly dominate the perception of CPAs by the public-at-large.

Why is this?

1. CPA work is technically demanding and requires lots of discipline. Many people lack the intellect and focus to excel at these tasks. People have a tendency to ridicule and make fun of others whom they envy or see as more successful than they are. Poking fun and demeaning CPAs "brings them down a level" to the common man.

2. A stereotype of public accounting has evolved over many decades: it's seen as dull, boring work requiring punishingly long hours chained to a desk. Stereotypes die hard - the longer they exist, the harder they are to change, even in the face of evidence to the contrary.

3. We live in an age of specialization. Attorneys, bankers and the business community at large understand what CPAs do and hold them in high regard. But the average "Joe" walking down the street has little or no understanding of CPAs and what they do.

Some of the image problem is our own fault

Many years ago, syndicated newspaper columnist Bob Greene wrote a piece that epitomized the role accountants play in perpetuating their own image problem. Entitled "Accountants Adopt Poor Self-Image," the vintage-1987 column is summarized below.

Greene began:

"A term that we have all heard tossed around in recent years is: "self-image." We have been told that certain lower echelon economic groups have poor self-images; that certain ethnic groups have poor self-images; that abused people often develop poor self-images. This is undoubtedly valid. The idea of a poor self-image can be a haunting thing, especially for a person who has done nothing to deserve it.

"But I recently ran into a group of people who had just about the worst self-images I have ever encountered. I was shocked. The self-images of these people were so pitiful that I felt like calling for a SWAT team of psychiatrists to help out.

"The people with the awful self-images: Accountants."

Greene explains he'd given a speech earlier that week at a Big Eight national convention; on Friday night he decides to stop for a drink at their annual dinner dance. Dressed like a "disreputable bum" in jeans, he discovers it's a formal affair and expects to be thrown out when accosted at the bar by partners in black tie. Instead, one says:

"I know, I know. You're going to write a column about us. What a bunch of nerds we are."

A second partner chimes in, "I know what you're going to write. 'The bean-counters try to have a wild time.' "

Another says, "Don't be too hard on us in your story. We may not be very exciting, but some of us are nice people."

107

Greene explains he'd had no intention of writing a column.
"What's wrong with you people? You're rich, you're successful, you've reached the top of your field...why do you feel this way about what you do? If I do decide to write a story, it's going to be about your self-images."

"No it won't," a partner says, "You'll just say that accountants are nerds."

Greene considers telling them that his own accountant is one of his favorite people but realizes no one will believe him. "By all rights I should have been tossed out of the party. And the partners of the firm were lining up to tell me they were sorry they seemed like nerds – when in fact, they didn't seem like nerds at all."

Finally a distinguished looking senior partner of the firm approaches Greene, looks him up and down and says, "We spend a million dollars for security at this convention, and then someone like you can just walk right in."

"I shook his hand," Greene concludes. "You're the sanest person I've met all night."

Moral of the story: CPAs do have an image problem, which is at least partly of their own making.

<u>Here's how the poor image "myth" gets perpetuated</u>

This piece illustrates how slanted the media can be sometimes.

YAHOO! HITS ACCOUNTANTS BELOW THE BELT

July 16, 2012. Yahoo! homepage printed an article "Six Careers For People Who Don't Like People." Heading the list was "Accountants." They quoted Nancy Ancowitz, a business coach and author of "Self Promotion for Introverts." Said Ancowitz: "Are you happier focusing on spreadsheets vs. listening to coworkers or customers talking all day? If so, consider a career accounting."

This article is an affront to all accountants who have been battling this image problem for decades. It enraged me. I wrote Ancowitz the following letter.

Dear Ms. Ancowitz:

I am writing this on behalf of the accounting community regarding your characterization of a career in accounting as "a great option for people who just want to be left alone," or as Yahoo! quotes your book, a "career for people who don't like people." You and Yahool! have both taken the easy path of succumbing to a tired view that typecasts accountants as number-crunchers who are people-averse.

I beg to differ.

CPAs' existence is founded on the cultivation and nurturing of strong relationships. A CPA can be brilliant in her work and incredibly innovative in counseling clients but these attributes are of little use if the CPA fails to establish a close working relationship with clients and inspiring leadership to the firm's staff. 90% of a CPA's *new* clients originate from *existing* clients and referral sources. Do you think these people would refer clients to a CPA who dislikes being with people?

Ask *clients* to describe their CPA. You'll hear things like: "One of the people I like best is my CPA" or "I can't think of anyone I **would** rather go out to dinner with than my CPA" or "My CPA plays a meaningful role in my life." The vast majority of CPA firms earn more revenue every year than they did the year before. Clients rarely fire their CPA firm. Would clients rehire their CPA year after year if they were anti-social?

Ask any successful CPA firm what attribute of their personnel is valued the highest. It's not brilliant accounting and tax knowledge. It's not rainmaking. It's not willingness to work long hours. <u>It's people skills.</u>

Thousands of Baby Boomer CPAs are approaching normal retirement age and choosing to continue working. It's not because of the money. It's not because their firm needs them to stay. It's because they enjoy what they do and the love affair they have with their clients. Does this sound like the kind of person who doesn't like being with people?

I'm quite sure that corporation CFOs and Treasurers would yield similar stories. Their stakeholders are their staffs, top management and key external people such as stockholders, investment bankers, attorneys and bankers. The careers of these people would have been doomed before they got started if they didn't like being with people.

In stereotyping accountants you have grouped yourself with:
- Blondes are stupid.
- Generals love war.
- Lawyers are shysters.
- Arabs are terrorists.
- The wealthy are elitist.
- Artists starve.

You get the picture. Sure, accountants have an image problem. Uninformed people might think of accountants as nerds. Well-informed people, including writers who do their research, know better.

Someone once said "an insult is the sincerest form of flattery."

Marc Rosenberg CPA

Before they were famous, they studied accounting

- John Grisham
- Mick Jagger
- Janet Jackson
- Bob Newhart
- Kenny G.
- J.P. Morgan
- Mick Tinglehoff, former center of Minnesota Vikings
- Kevin Kennedy, former manager of Texas Rangers

After the elections of November, 2012, there were 10 members in the House that are CPAs, including:

- Brad Sherman of California (D)
- Tom Rice of South Carolina (R)
- Mike Conaway of Texas (R)
- Bill Flores of Texas (R)
- Lynn Jenkins of Kansas (R)
- Steven Palazzo of Mississippi (R)
- Collin Peterson of Minnesota (D)
- John Campbell of California (R)
- James Renacci of Ohio (R)

14

Accountants in the Movies

I realize this chapter title may elicit some chuckles. The accountant as matinee idol seems an oxymoron if there ever was one.

The good news is that, in fact, there have been many movies made with accountants playing an important role. If you don't believe me, Google "accountants in the movies" and before your eyes, dozens of movie titles will appear.

The bad news is that in virtually all cases, the accountant plays the stereotypical number-crunching nerd that we laugh *at* and would never call "cool."

Now, you will have to grant me a certain amount of poetic license when I say these movies *feature* accountants, but the memorable scenes I've highlighted are right up the accountant's proverbial alley.

So, here are my personal favorites. Every one of these movies is a great movie, over and above the role played by an accountant. If you've never seen them, I highly recommend them all.

Dave	
Stars: Kevin Kline Sigourney Weaver Frank Langella 	**Story line:** The president falls into a coma and his staff look for someone who looks exactly like him to "fill in" until he recovers. They find their man, Dave, the owner of a temp agency in a small town. The shady chief of staff seizes the opportunity to ram legislation through Congress and instructs the President's stand-in, Dave, to be quiet and do as he's told, frequently reminding him in very hostile ways that he is <u>not</u> the President. But Dave likes being President and changes the country for the better.

Memorable scene: Dave struggles to find room in the federal budget for important bills. Out of desperation, he calls his CPA, Murray Blum, to the White House to review the books. The great scene has Dave and Murray at a conference table in the Oval Office, strewn with papers and computer printouts. An exasperated Murray says: "I've been over these books a thousand times and they just don't add up. If I ran my business the way the country runs theirs, I'd be out of business."

Ghostbusters	
Stars: Bill Murray Dan Aykroyd Sigourney Weaver Rick Moranis 	**Story line:** Three scientists form a business to exterminate ghosts and evil spirits. They stumble upon a gateway to another dimension in an apartment building that will unleash untold evil upon NYC. The Ghostbusters are called in to save the day.

Memorable scene: Rick Moranis, an accountant, tries to woo a neighbor in his apartment building, the glamorous Sigourney Weaver. The building is haunted and Moranis comes under a hypnotic spell cast by the devil himself. But the Ghostbusters save the day and eradicate the devil. A besieged Moranis snaps out of his spell on the roof of the building in front of Murray and Aykroyd (the Ghostbusters), both of whom are covered from head to foot with white, marshmallow-like slime. With his tell-tale black glasses seated crookedly across his nose, hair and clothes a mess, Moranis looks at the odd-looking Ghostbusters for about 5 seconds in silence. Then, still wobbly from the effects of the spell, he says in a broken voice: "Who does your taxes?"

Hitch	
Stars: Will Smith Kevin James 	**Story line:** Will Smith is the super-cool "date doctor" who helps men land dates. Kevin James is the bumbling, clumsy overweight young tax consultant at a CPA firm who dreams of falling in love with the firm's biggest client, a young billionaire heiress that is drop-dead gorgeous. She knows nothing of his affection for her.

Memorable scene: In a meeting with the heiress and 5 senior members of his firm, James gets up his nerve to make a suggestion that the old men immediately ridicule. But she stops their criticism by saying she really likes the idea. This instantly changes the partners' demeanor from scowls to smiles. When the meeting breaks up, James marches back to his office to fill in the "date doctor" on what just happened. After a few moments, there is a knock on his office door and standing there is the heiress. She tells James how much she appreciated him standing up for her in the meeting and asks if they could get together later in the week, "you know, to go over things, financial things. I'd like to see the areas where I can take some risk." In a hilarious scene, Will Smith, who is unseen behind the open door, coaches James, who is in shock and practically speechless. Smith coaches James with a variety of hand signals and facial gestures. The scene ends with her giving James her card and asking him to call her.

Honeymooners	
Stars: Jackie Gleason Art Carney 	**Story line:** In this episode, Ralph receives a letter from the IRS, summoning him to a meeting in 10 days' time. In typical Ralph Kramden fashion, he obsesses about what he could have done wrong and what will happen to him. His wife Alice admonishes him: "I told you to take your tax return to the barber like everyone else but you did it yourself." So Ralph calls on his best friend and expert on everything, Ed Norton, for help.

Memorable scene: First, Ralph and Norton sit at the kitchen table, pouring over the 1040, trying to identify what he did wrong. Norton, reading the instructions, asks if Ralph reported the $85 he won while gambling. Ralph says "No. Do you think they found out about that?" Norton says: "Now that's the kind of item they're investigating you for." The scene shifts to Ralph arriving at the IRS. When the agent walks in, Ralph blabbers: "I didn't do it." The agent responds: "Of course you didn't do it. That's why we called you down here. Your signature. You didn't sign your tax form."

Intolerable Cruelty	
Stars: George Clooney Catherine Zeta-Jones 	**Story line:** Clooney is a high-powered divorce attorney who has everything: Money. Fame. Prestige. Social stature. Despite having everything, he reaches a crossroads in his life, kind of a mid-life crisis. Just then, he meets his match in the devastating Zeta-Jones . Her divorce case drags on and on until he is summoned into the office of Herb, the firm's revered but dreaded senior partner.
Memorable scene: Clooney sits outside the senior partner's office and randomly grabs a magazine. After nervously leafing through a few pages, he flips to the cover: *Life Without Intestines.* As Clooney slowly walks into Herb's office, the camera fixes on a man who seems to be at least 100, sitting behind his desk in a 3-piece suit, tubes leading into every part of his body. Herb rants, gasping for air between each sentence: "85 lunches charged. 1221 motions to void. 564 summary judgments. 320 billable hours." Then, when Clooney reaches his desk, Herb says: "You are the engine that drives this firm."	

Jerry Maguire	
Stars: Tom Cruise Cuba Gooding Jr. Renee Zellweger 	**Story line:** Maguire, played by Cruise, is a successful sports agent in a big firm. He starts questioning the ethics and purpose of his work. His firm doesn't appreciate this change of heart and he is forced to leave the firm. He leaves without any clients except possibly one: a volatile football player (Gooding) who wants a new contract with his team. Maguire desperately tries everything he can think of to retain this client.
Memorable scene: Gooding is in the kitchen of his home with his family, talking on the phone with Cruise, who is desperate to find out if Gooding will retain him. Gooding: "I have a family to support. I want to stay in Arizona. I want a new contract. We like you Jerry. I will stay with you. That's what I'm going to do for you. Now, here's what I want from you. It's a very personal, important thing. It's a family motto. SHOW ME THE MONEY." What follows is a hilarious back and forth with Gooding imploring Cruise to yell this refrain over and over again, louder and louder each time. The scene ends with Gooding saying, in a calm voice: "Congratulations Jerry. You're still my agent."	

L.A. Story	
Stars: Steve Martin Sarah Jessica Parker Patrick Stewart 	**Story line:** Martin is a weekend weatherman searching for a new meaning in his cliché ridden L.A. life. He has a girlfriend who is dominating, egotistical and boring. He meets a 20-something girl in a clothing store who he falls for and she asks him to take her to dinner at the latest, trendy, French restaurant: L'Idiot (pronounced in French, of course). He calls for a reservation and after hearing raucous laughter on the other end, is told that to qualify for a reservation, he must first meet the restaurant's owner and chef at a bank.

Memorable scene: At the bank, Martin is seated at a conference table with the bank officer, the restaurant owner (Stewart) and the chef. The banker says "the owner is looking for more than a promise to pay. He's looking for a certain depth in your financial sea." The owner continues: "Suppose we give you a reservation. What would you order?" Martin sheepishly says "the duck." The chef immediately says, with a thick French accent: "He cannot have the duck." The owner repeats it. When Martin asks why, the owner holds up a computer printout and says angrily: "Do you think with financial statements like this, you can have the duck?" The chef says: "He can have the CHEE-kun."

Monty Python	
Stars: John Cleese Michael Palin 	**Story line:** Cleese is the HR director of a company. An accountant at the company, Palin, is asking for a change in jobs. He says he wants something exciting, something that will let him live.

Memorable scene: Cleese asks Palin why he wants to change jobs. Palin says he wants something more interesting. Cleese begins leafing through Palin's personnel file and says: "It says here that you are an extremely dull person. Our experts describe you as an appallingly dull fellow, timid, lacking in initiative, tedious, easily dominated, spineless, no sense of humor and depressively drab and awful. Whereas in most professions, these would be considerable drawbacks, in Chartered Accountancy, they are a positive boon."

117

The Closet

Stars:	Story line: This movie is the sleeper among the films
A French movie; no recognizable stars. 	described in this chapter. A bland accountant at a rubber factory has just been divorced by his wife, who detests him. His teenage son sees his father as a nerd. Rumors circulate in the company that there will be layoffs, and the accountant fears he will be fired. To prevent this, he spreads the rumor that he is gay so that the company's management might be afraid they'll be sued for sexual discrimination if they fire him.

Memorable scene: The man's co-workers now see him differently, and are strangely impressed by his courage to come out of the closet, daring to be different. He works with two women in the accounting department, both young and beautiful, one of which is his boss, the controller. She asks him to work late one evening to finish the balance sheet. Over Chinese food in the accounting office, late that night, the controller engages the man in conversation about himself. The controller says she sees through his crafty ploy and knows he's not gay, which the man does not deny. One thing leads to another and before you know it, they are making passionate love on the conference table. At just the "right moment," the President, leading a tour of the plant for a group of Japanese businessmen, sees the two feverishly grappling with each other on the table. All the men stare, mouths agape. The quick-witted President tells the Japanese: "And those...those are our testers."

The Producers

Stars:	Story line: A down-and-out theatre producer
Zero Mostel; Gene Wilder 	(Mostel) is visited by his accountant, Leo Bloom, (Wilder). In reviewing the books, Wilder discovers serious fraud and tells Mostel he could go to jail if anyone finds out.

Memorable scene: Mostel goes berserk. "Come on. Move a few decimal points around. You can do it. You're an accountant. You're in a noble profession. The word 'count' is in your title." After repeated pleading from Mostel, Wilder reluctantly agrees to hide the fraud. As he starts fudging the books, a thought occurs to the accountant. "Under the right circumstances, a producer could make more money from a flop than a hit. It's simply a matter of creative accounting." They proceed to pour over a pile of lousy manuscripts until they find the perfect, sure-fire flop: "Springtime for Hitler."

Shawshank Redemption	
Stars: Tim Robbins Morgan Freeman 	**Story line:** Robbins plays a young and successful banker/accountant who is convicted and sentenced to life imprisonment for the murder of his wife and her lover. The film shows how Robbins lives through his incarceration with the help of his friend and fellow prisoner, Red (Freeman), the prison entrepreneur.

Memorable scene: The cruel, crooked prison captain is watching over a group of inmates tarring a building roof. The captain reveals to a fellow guard that he just inherited $35,000 from his brother. But he's unhappy because "the government will take most of it in taxes." Robbins overhears this, drops his mop, slowly walks over to the captain and asks: "Do you trust your wife." The captain immediately grabs him by the collar and starts dragging him to the edge of the roof, while Robbins yells out: "If you trust her, there's no reason you should pay taxes on the $35,000." As they reach the roof's edge, the captain says: "Start making sense." With the captain's hands still on his neck, Robbins explains: "You can give the money to your wife because the IRS allows a one-time only gift to your wife. It's perfectly legal. I suppose I could set it up for you. If you get the forms, I'll prepare them for you. Free of charge."

The Untouchables	
Stars: Kevin Kostner Charles Martin Smith 	**Story line:** Most accountants know the story – the only way the Chicago police were able to put Al Capone in prison was not from any convictions for murder or bootlegging, but from tax evasion. Kostner plays Eliot Ness and Smith, type-cast throughout his career as a short, wimpy nerd, is sent by the government to join Ness's special crime team.

Memorable scene: Smith is waiting in Eliot Ness's office, sitting as Ness's desk, as Kostner (Ness) arrives to work one morning. Smith introduces himself, saying that the FBI sent him to help. Kostner, clearly unaware of this, says he certainly would be interested in any ideas he has. Smith proudly says he has one. As he leafs through a stack of files on the desk, he triumphantly pounds his hand on a document and proclaims: "Capone hasn't filed a return since 1926." Kostner says incredulously: "What do you *do* at the Bureau?" Smith responds: "Oh, I'm an accountant." Kostner says, "An accountant huh. I see." Bewildered, Kostner then excuses himself, motions to Smith to reclaim the desk chair and continue his work as he walks out of his office, shaking his head.

119

Schindler's List	
Stars: Liam Neeson Ben Kingsley Ralph Fiennes 	**Story line:** Based on a true story. Oskar Schindler (Neeson) is a vainglorious German businessman who becomes an unlikely humanitarian to the Jews during the Holocaust. He turns his factory into an arms manufacturing plant and employs Jews as the free labor force, and in the process, provides them a refuge for from the concentration camps. He enlists one of the Jew's leaders (Kingsley) to be his general manager and accountant.

Memorable scene: Kingsley is quite understandably nervous for his life as he sees a continuous stream of Jews marched out of the ghetto to concentration camps. He wonders when his turn will come. Schindler leads Kingsley into an office and tells of his grand plan, saying: "I want you to run the company." Stunned by this offer, Kingsley responds: "Let me understand. The Nazis put up all the money and I do all the work. If you don't mind my asking, what will *you* do?" Schindler responds: "I take care of our relationship with the government. I'd see that our factory had a certain...panache. That's what I'm good at. Not the work. It's all about...the presentation."

Here are a few other movies featuring accountants. The star playing the accountant is in parentheses.

- Civil Action (William H. Macy)
- Moonstruck (Cher)
- Same Time Next Year (Alan Alda)
- Stranger Than Fiction (Will Ferrell)
- Carnal Knowledge (Jack Nicholson)
- Cheers (George Wendt's character "Norm)

15

Top 20 Reasons Clients Love Their CPA Firms

The CPA's training is geared to identifying problems that clients are experiencing and giving recommendations for improving the company. This leads to producing what is known as the "Oh wow" feeling from a client. Efforts to super-please clients are what it takes to satisfy clients' needs, retain them year after year and get them to make unsolicited referrals of other companies.

Here are 20 things that CPAs do that their clients rave about:

1. **CPAs help their clients save or make money.** Examples: lowering income taxes, making wise lease vs. buy decisions, doing estate planning and analyzing the purchase of businesses and equipment.

2. **CPAs give their clients good ideas.** The ideas come whether the clients ask for them or not. And the CPA will give it to the client straight, even if he/she doesn't like what is heard.

3. **CPAs have expertise in various industries.** A small minority of clients are uncomfortable that their CPA firm may have 20 other clients in the same industry. But most appreciate the specialized expertise their CPA firm can provide them *because* of their experience in working with similar businesses.

121

4. **CPAs are their clients' most trusted advisors.** CPAs can be counted on for integrity, honesty, moral behavior and trust more than any other professionals that clients work with. That's why their clients consider them to be their most trusted advisor.

CPAs can be relied upon for a diverse array of services that their clients badly need. Gone are the days when a company's expectations of their CPA firm were limited to performing the audit or preparing a tax return. There is so much more that CPA firms offer: wealth management, mergers and acquisitions, business valuations, estate planning, personal financial planning, forensic investigations, R&D credits – the list goes on.

5. **CPAs are hardworking.** They work crazy hours throughout the year to meet client deadlines. They go the extra mile to please the client. When clients call with a crisis, be it at night or on a weekend, the CPA is always willing to help. Clients come first to CPAs, often at great sacrifice to their own families.

6. **CPAs provide strategic advice.** What business should I be in? How should I price my products? What direction is my business headed? How should I organize my company? What are my goals? These are the types of issues that CPAs help their clients with every day.

7. **CPAs "know" people.** CPAs are the quarterbacks of the business world. If they can't do it themselves, CPAs know others who can. CPAs have contacts with other professionals – attorneys, bankers, insurance agents, money managers, etc. Clients trust their CPAs to give them good referrals.

8. **CPAs charge reasonable fees.** There are some who would argue that this is not a positive. But clients rarely feel ripped off by their CPAs. When clients open the envelope containing their CPA's bills, they rarely get a big surprise. This doesn't mean that the CPA's fees are low or that they are cheap. The best CPAs have their clients say this about them: "My CPA firm is expensive, but they're good!"

9. **CPAs keep you informed.** Clients can count on their CPAs to keep them informed of tax and other developments that affect their business. Many firms send informative newsletters to their clients on a regular basis. When CPAs read an article that applies to clients, they will email it to them.

10. **CPAs introduce you to people you should know.** With many CPAs, referrals aren't made in just one direction. CPAs will introduce clients to potential customers, vendors and other contacts.

11. **CPAs save your _*ss_!** Clients find themselves in messes from time to time. IRS audits. Structuring deals. Getting bank loans. You name it. CPAs are great at resolving dicey problems for their clients.

12. **CPAs have a back-up.** If a company's main partner contact is not available and an important matter comes up, clients know others at the firm to call. Whether its staff assigned to the client or another partner, the lead partner usually has a back-up.

13. **CPAs offer a diversity of services.** In addition to traditional accounting and tax services, CPAs help their clients install computers, analyze acquisitions, make sound investments, procure bank loans, recruit controllers and much more.

14. **CPAs and Disney have the same mission statements.** Disney's mission is "making millions happy." Disney's theme parks are legendary for attention to detail in the pursuit of super-pleasing their customers. CPAs have an uncompromising dedication to providing world class service as well. Making profits is nowhere in the mission statement of Disney or CPA firms; if a company "makes millions happy," profits will come.

15. **CPAs are accessible.** Lawyers are always busy due to their billable hour mentality. Doctors are always busy seeing patients assembled in a continuous row of examining rooms. But CPAs are usually pretty easy to reach. Clients like that.

16. CPAs are stable. CPA firm partners don't move around much. It's common for CPAs to be with the same firm for decades. CPAs are in it for the long haul.

17. CPAs are nice people. Despite their reputation as introverts, CPAs are also described as the kind of people that others look forward to having dinner with, or inviting to their children's weddings. The vast majority are bright, caring, interesting people who leave their egos at the doorstep.

18. CPAs give their clients peace of mind. For the 1040 client, CPA firms help with estate planning, college financing, reducing income taxes and a myriad of other personal financial problems. For businesses, CPA firms can be the calm, objective advisors that hold the ship together in the face of the unexpected resignation of a dynamite controller or a devastating emergency.

19. ...and oh yes...CPAs are good accountants and tax specialists. Make no mistake about it. This is their bread and butter.

20. CPAs make their clients' lives better. For the 19 reasons listed above. Good CPAs are worth their weight in gold.

Staff Quiz

1. **For over 30 years, the Gallup organization has conducted periodic polls of the public's perception of the honesty & ethics of various professions. How do accountants compare to other professions?**

	Public's Perception of Accountants vs. Other Professions
Accountants	43%
Journalists	26%
Bankers	25%
Lawyers	19%
Stock brokers	12%

Correct answer: Accountants rate way higher than all of them. Accountants have scored highly in honesty and ethics since the survey began. We took a hit in the aftermath of the Enron/Andersen fiascos in 2001, going down to 32% from 42% just prior to these events. But within a year, the rating began steadily increasing until, in 2011, the last year of this poll, the rating surpassed the pre-Enron score, and currently is 43%.

The percentages cited above represents the percentage of people that rated each profession as "very high" or "high."

2. **What is the #1 practice management trend in the CPA profession today?**

   Correct answer: Succession planning. The retirement of huge numbers of Baby Boomer partners at multi-partner firms or sole practitioners and have no younger partners to take their place, has spawned a mammoth succession planning crisis in the CPA profession. This is a world-wide phenomenon.

3. **How many total work hours (including overtime, non-billable time, sick, vacation and holiday time) does the average _staff_ person at a CPA firm work?**

   Correct answer: 2,257. This equates to roughly 200 hours of overtime. Is that a lot? Is that too much? Does that make a career in public accounting undesirable? It depends on who you ask.

   Someone who wants no part of working overtime had best not consider a career in public accounting. But I would challenge anyone to name one profession or career that offers challenge and responsibility along with good pay, that does not require _some_ overtime.

4. **How many total work hours does the average _partner_ at a CPA firm work?**

   Correct answer: 2,413. Is that a lot? Is that too much? Does working 2,413 hours prevent someone from achieving a desirable work/life balance? Again, it depends on whom you ask and what standard of living you want.

   Those who conclude that it's virtually impossible to have a decent work/life balance should talk with the thousands of CPA firm partners I have had the pleasure of knowing. These are people who found plenty of time to have a challenging career, lead a great family life, coach their kid's soccer teams, be active in the community and take lots of vacations. 333 overtime hours does not a workaholic make. By any stretch.

A few years ago, I led a focus group of young staff from 15 Chicago area CPA firms. I asked them how many hours they think their partners work. Their responses averaged 2,900. The staff felt that the partners seem to work "all the time." Obviously, they were greatly mistaken. Partners need to be careful to perpetuate a workaholic image that disillusions staff.

5. **What is the average income of a typical equity partner at a local CPA firm?**

Correct answer: $360,000. Using data from the IRS's data bank, that's higher than 98% of all people. Pretty darned good, I would say.

6. **What is the single most important skill, talent or attribute that it takes to become a partner at a CPA firm?**

Correct answer: Interpersonal skills. I'm sure I'll get some arguments on this one. Some would debate that bringing in business and technical knowledge would be most important. But I give the nod to interpersonal skills because ultimately, this will determine your success. The ability to interact positively and effectively with others almost always is the key differentiator in one's career. This entails communicating, listening, leadership, delegation and supervision. In a CPA firm, the importance of earning the trust and credibility of clients, firm personnel and referral sources is undeniable.

Partner Quiz

1. **For over 30 years, the Gallup organization has conducted periodic polls of the public's perception of the honesty and ethics of various professions. How do you think accountants compare to other professions?**

    Answer: Accountants have a higher perception for honesty and ethics than all of the professions listed: Bankers, journalists, lawyers and stock brokers.

    See question #1 answer a few pages earlier in the staff quiz.

2. **Name 3 "game-changing" innovations in the CPA firm industry during the past 20 years besides technology.**

    Answer:
    *   Shift in focus from clients to staff.
    *   Proactive marketing of CPA firm services.
    *   Business consulting added to CPA portfolio of accounting & tax.
    *   Specialization and niche marketing.

3. **Name 3 overarching trends in the CPA firm industry today. Limit your choices to management issues vs. technical issues.**

    Answer:
    *   Shortage of staff
    *   Massive retirement of Baby Boomer partners
    *   Succession planning crisis
    *   Mergers- tons of them

4. **For most local, multi-partner firms, the best and easiest opportunity to increase revenues is (check only one):**

    [ ] Referral sources
    [ ] Advertising, PR and branding
    [x] **Existing clients**

5. The strongest correlation with firm profitability is (check only one):

[ ] Overhead spending   [ ] Partner charge hours
[ ] Staff charge hours   [x] **Fees per partner**

6. Which of the following are among the <u>most important</u> factors in <u>retaining</u> staff at a CPA firm (check all that are most important):

[ ] Firm's reputation and prestige
[x] **Career growth opportunities**
[x] **Salary and benefits**
[x] **Interesting, challenging projects**
[ ] Telecommuting & work from home options

Made in the USA
Charleston, SC
11 January 2014